Patricia Holland is a writer, filmmaker and the visiting tutor on the postgraduate diploma on Media and Communications at Goldsmiths College, University of London. Her independent production *What are schools for?* is distributed by Metro Films. She has contributed to various academic journals and books and co-edited *Photography/Politics Two* (Comedia 1986) and *Family Snaps* (Virago 1990).

Patricia Holland

What is a child?

Popular images of childhood

Learning Resources
Centre

Published by VIRAGO PRESS Ltd 1992
20–23 Mandela Street, Camden Town, London NW1 0HQ

A CIP catalogue record for this book is available from the British Library

Design by Arthur Lockwood
Typeset by Goodfellow & Egan Phototypesetting Ltd, Cambridge
Printed in Great Britain

 1853812730

Contents

5

Acknowledgements

The idea for this book grew out of the exhibition *Children Photographed* mounted in 1976 by Jo Spence and Andrew Mann of the Children's Rights Workshop, and Christine Vincent, Diana Phillips and Arthur Lockwood of the design group Ikon. Their work in collecting and discussing pictures of children over the intervening years has made an invaluable contribution to the final book.

I should also like to thank Vicki Annand for access to her extensive collection of pictures of children and Katrin Anderson for many interesting conversations on the subject of children and childhood.

Introduction

Pictures of children: images of childhood

Sense and sensuality for our times

This book is about pictures of children and the public imagery of childhood. It is about the stories woven by that imagery and the visual delight it brings. It is about the dream of childhood and its persistent nightmare. The communications industries provide a repertoire of visual excitement that is dazzling yet mundane. Pictures on the page or screen, easy and unemphatic in their omnipresence and attractiveness, feed comfortably into the common sense of our age. They express emotion, challenge or confirm ideas, re-present to us the world and our place in it, evoke the delights of visual display. They form a populous world of two dimensions, threaded through our living world of flesh and blood.

The kaleidoscope of this urban image world is unique to twentieth-century experience. An arrogant assertion of social wealth, it is also an irremovable part of the way we make our meanings. It is an imagery in use. We use it to name the world and to position individuals in different ways within that world. Children hold a special place in this imagery of our times. The engaging smile, the mischievous grin, the pout, the tear, the expression of joys forgotten to adulthood – we greet these beguiling pictures with a special sort of pleasure as they circulate in the public spaces of our decaying inner cities, our spruced-up country towns and our suburban shopping parades. Childhood lends itself to spectacular presentation.

I shall be looking at public pictures which help to create our collective image of childhood and asking: who claims the right to produce these images, who constructs their meanings, what sort of claim do they make to authenticity and truth, and what is the importance of a challenge to that claim? The moving pictures of television and the cinema are excluded – not because they are unimportant, but because they are possibly *too* important and have deflected attention away from the still image, which has its own special qualities. I shall not be considering the work of particular photographers or graphic artists but look at public imagery as a total phenomenon, something that is made up not of singular, precious pictures but of multiples in time and space, each picture reduplicated thousands, if not millions, of times. The images circulate between the media, echoing back and forth: from newspapers to advertisements, from the pages of magazines to postcards, packaging and wrapping paper.

Professional image-makers are greedy for material. Even the precious objects of art history lose what Walter Benjamin called their 'aura' – their unique presence in time and space – and enter the public arena in endless recapitulation. A repertoire of reference and self-reference is built up. Groups of pictures cluster together, gaining meaning from their proximity and their continuous reference to each other. The meanings of any one picture or visual representation are never complete because they always refer to other pictures and other texts. They are never finally established and can always be reused in a new way. Public imagery carries its meanings only within this total context.

The very ubiquity of these pictures means that we treat them with careless disregard. Magazines, sweet wrappers, greetings cards are waste paper that can be screwed up in the hand or discarded in the dustbin. Advertising hoardings can be whisked past at car speed or hurried past on foot. Yet our public imagery as such remains virtually indestructible, its presence insistent and beyond our control. Any individual item may be disregarded, but as one is thrown away, another, similar if not identical, is instantly to hand. Each picture remains, half remembered, an impression only, difficult to find again once lost and yet as familiar as if it were always present. So, when we isolate a news photo or an advertisement for critical comment, it can hardly bear the weight of the study. How can one or even a dozen pictures represent that massive flow which permeates our everyday experience? Any discussion of public imagery must take into account this persistent yet ephemeral quality.

This proliferation of imagery does not necessarily mean an equal proliferation of sense. The pictures are always different, always shifting – but as we look at them more closely, we find a constant attempt to buttonhole viewers, to pin them down and trap them within a limited field of meaning. Instead of allowing space for understanding to develop, we find attempts to secure meanings within a structure of power and establish their own regimes of truth. We find a denial of ambiguity, a fear of interpretations which may run way out of control. The exciting variety of the visual surface may serve to distract from the insistent repetition of the conceptual message.

The imagery classifies, sorts and labels, attempting to hold fast meanings which will be clear and uncontaminated. Pictures of children take their place in this complex system like words in a language, held in place by their difference from other signs in the system. The children in Kodak advertisements and on cornflakes packets stand not for this or that particular child but for aspects of childhood itself in a way that can seem independent of human intervention. The pictures establish contrasts and distinctions, separating children from adults, boys from girls.

Key images emerge which condense into themselves the most emphatic of such meanings – the wide eyes of the appealing child, the crouched body of the abused child, the structured placing of the child within the family. The implications of such images resonate across the range of imagery. Public pictures create a pictorial vocabulary.

But a picture can only affirm. Unlike a sentence, it cannot express doubt or pose a question. It waits for language to unsettle it. Presentations of public imagery characteristically combine pictures and text, relying on the exchange of meanings between the two. The text directs us how to read the picture, and the picture can act to externalise meanings and make them more concrete. Its affirmative quality can pre-empt questioning, and offer an assurance that language seems powerless to contradict. Pictures seem to halt the slipperiness of language, pull meanings together and bind them so that they appear natural and irresistible. The abstract signifier of verbal language is given shape by the mental imagery of pictorial communication. A concept like that of childhood is always partly visual.

Pictures on a page call up images in our minds. Pictures of children, images of childhood. The tangible representation evokes the shadowy concept which is neither purely visual nor entirely verbal. Sometimes it is inseparable from the picture, sometimes it may be evoked by language. Sometimes it seems to stand alone, partly verbal, partly pictorial, taking its place amongst the social expectations of our time. A resonant image generates in its turn new pictures for our use. But this is not a system we can detach ourselves from or step outside. A formal analysis will always be inadequate, for it touches our very sense of ourselves and our place in the world.

Pictures of children are part of a set of interweaving narratives of childhood which are both public and private, and personal and social. These narratives without an author explore such themes as family, sexuality, nature, schooling and violence. Built up across different cultural forms, they draw on every possible source to construct the stories that become part of our cultural competence. We ourselves become joint authors of those stories as we experience the pleasure of recognition, and look to them for guidance on our behaviour and relationships. In an entertaining way we take part in the mapping of our social, political and emotional worlds. With their audience's collaboration, the narratives of the public media set up patterns of expectation which sediment into the half-conscious cultural understandings of our time. They construct a set of patterns within the dominant political and economic system which makes it possible to carry out our daily lives and commit ourselves to meaningful actions. At the same time our most personal stories, our memories, the tales we tell ourselves about ourselves, are shaped and inflected by the public imagery and public narratives we have available to us. These stories become our stories, these pictures our pictures.

But there is always something more. The visual enables a static moment which interrupts the eager flow of the narrative and the incessant demands of understanding. Imagery gives us pause, offers a time out, however short, from the insistent flow. It may be a moment of celebration, of unquestioning affirmation or it may be a moment of hesitation and disturbance, allowing the otherwise inexpressible to be hinted at. Pictures offer both reality and illusion. They are both more representational than language and more fantastic. A picture can pull a moment out from the passage of time and hold it static for our delight. It can offer us visions – of places we have never visited, people we will never meet, experiences we have only dreamt of, fantasies the more powerful for their seeming reality. Pictures act in what appear to be contradictory ways. Sometimes they seem like a window on the world, separating us from it, enabling us to observe and hence control it. At other times they act as a mirror in which we see ourselves reflected so that we seem to become an inseparable part of the scene before us. When we look in a mirror we gaze at our faces, searching for the reflected image of our ideal selves. In public pictures a model, an abstract individual, someone in an advertisement who represents no one in the real world, may serve very well for that ideal, and help us imagine ourselves as we would love to be. Pictures, then, seem to clarify experience and enhance the value of our lives. They offer material for constructing and reconstructing our own lives and making judgements on those of others. The same anonymous child in the picture may on some occasions seem like an indulgent view of our earlier selves; on others like an obstreperous son or daughter pushing their luck. These various ways of experiencing visual representations: reflecting an ideal self, expressing emotion, controlling others – different modes that are nevertheless constantly transforming themselves into each other – are all part of the potent imagery of childhood.

The division between the spectacular and the conceptual is not merely a division between pictures and words. A tension arises within the image itself between our enjoyment of a picture and our comprehension of it. The power of the spectacle resists any attempt to reduce it to verbal sense. It puts pressure on understanding in ways that language cannot deal with. Its emotional charge can open up unpredictable vistas. Always offering something more, always reaching towards the unconscious, the work of the spectacular cannot easily be accounted for. So although in one sense pictures pin down and concretise language, in another they add an irreducible ambiguity. The appealing eyes and puckered mouths of the children in the Kodak advertisements stir a different part of our consciousness. Conceptual meanings cannot be constructed without the repression of the inconvenient, the contradictory, that which is too disturbing. The spectacular allows such material to be expressed, without demanding to be recognised. It ensures that even in their realist modes, pictures never merely reflect the world around us. The imagery always draws on and nourishes the fantasy world of our longings. It mediates between our memory and our dreams. The nostalgia of imagery is part of the nostalgia each of us feels for a lost moment of satisfaction and a longing for a future of reconciliation and peace. This is a theme to which the imagery of childhood is well suited.

Cheated of childhood?

The image world displays and circulates countless pictures of children in everyday, routine usage. Making sense of them is part of a continuous adult effort to gain control over childhood and its implications – both over actual children and over a personal childhood which we are constantly mourning and constantly reinventing.

The multiple narratives of childhood built up by the imagery are far from consistent as they move between the different contexts of commerce, information and welfare. But as they play the image, recurring themes can be identified, echoing back and forth between them. The familiar typology of childhood includes the energetic boy and the seductive girl, the dependent child in need of protection, the ignorant child in need of education, the playful child in the home and the violent child on the streets. Sometimes pictures of children differentiate sharply between girls and boys; at other times the signifiers of age dominate those of gender. Some images are well developed, with many variations, but others appear less frequently and fit uneasily into the patterns of public presentation.

Above all, the imagery displays the social and psychic effort that goes into negotiating the difficult distinction between adult and child, to keep childhood separate from an adulthood that can never be fully achieved. Attempts are made to establish dual and opposing categories and hold them firm, in a dichotomy set against the actual continuity of growth and development. There is an active struggle to maintain childhood – if not actual children – as pure and uncontaminated. The ultimate, if paradoxical, fear is that children will be

ARE OUR CHILDREN GROWING UP TOO FAST?

WOMAN'S OWN – FIRST FOR CARING

Cute, isn't she? Dressed up in Mum's clothes, looking ever so sweet. It goes on in a million homes up and down the country. And it worries our own Claire Rayner. In their rush to grow up, are our children losing out? Read on, then tell us what you think

How did you react to the picture on this page? Did you look at it and think, 'Ah . . . how sweet! A little girl playing at being her mummy—it's lovely.' Or did you feel a vague distaste, an uneasiness at the sight of a small, very much prepubertal child dolled up in the trappings of a very much post-pubertal, indeed sexual, adult?

These days, more and more people react with dislike to the sight of children aping adults. The recent publicising of that long existing but hitherto hidden fact of life, the sexual abuse of children, has sensitised more and more of us to the symbolic messages being sent to adults about children by the clothes they wear.

When a little girl of three is sent out on the beach in not just a minuscule bikini bottom, but also a bikini top to cover her non-existent breasts, adults are being told: 'This child has sexual potential.' (And it's interesting by the way, that such ambivalence between child and adult does not exist in little boys' clothing. Only little girls are used in this way.)

When small children are dressed up in scaled-down copies of adult clothes and sent out to ape adult pursuits for entertainment, as in stage shows and formation danc-ing teams, and advertisements designed to make us buy goods, many of us feel uneasy. Are these children simply being used—or are they being abused?

And when at Christmas the shops fill up with kits of make-up and hairdressing gear for little girls, and dolls to be played with by being dressed and titivated to make them suitable small part-ners for their matching boyfriend dolls, there are many of us who reject them, crying, 'Leave our chil-dren alone! Let them stay children as long as they need to.'

And yet, children have to learn to be adults, and the way they do that is by imitation. Children who are never around adults, who are locked away in special baby places, fail to mature. They can't cope with adult life because they have no model for it. It is vital that children copy us from an early age. So we have a dilemma.

In fact, there has been a good deal of discussion in recent years about the sorts of models children are both given and encouraged to copy. Toys that are gender-orien-ted—dolls and toy cookers and cleaning equipment for little girls,

cars and guns and bows and arrows and so forth for boys—are distinctly out of fashion. Our chil-dren, modern teaching tells us, need to be given activities which are not aimed at brainwashing their small minds into thinking that girls are born to be grown-ups who cook and clean and look after babies, and boys to be grown-ups who swagger and drive cars and fight each other. Both sexes are capable of all sorts of activities and both need to be allowed to copy adults doing all of them if they are to learn how to live.

And that means they need to be allowed to dress up in adult clothes and pretend to be grown-ups. But no-one, not even the most radical of teachers, suggests boys should dress as adult women, or girls as adult men. Here it is tacitly accepted there should be sexual differences. And, in fact, every nursery and primary school class has its Wendy house and its dress-ing-up boxes to enable children to behave like adults of different sexes, if of similar abilities, and no-one thinks that at all wrong.

Which brings me back to pic-tures like the one on this page. If it is, in fact, a necessary part of a child's development to pretend to be Mummy, why is it that it makes some people—including, I cannot deny, me—so uneasy?

Can any of us feel easy seeing pop star Madonna using a young boy as part of her stage act? Isn't there a sense of loss when our own pre-leenage children don't want to be girls or boys any more but—that awful and cold term now in com-mon use—young adults?

Well, it grieves me and, I sus-pect, many parents. They suffer from what I call seven o'clock shock—the time when their chil-dren emerge from their bedrooms looking almost like 18-year-olds when, just hours before, they'd come home from school, Biro-stained and normal. And, of course, a whole industry has grown up to cater for the trans-formation where the message seems to be: 'Don't be kids any more, grow up fast!'

It's not a new problem but it is new in its intensity and it is new in that there seems no escape. And it's that, surely, which should make all of us uneasy!

■ Well, how do you feel? Write to Child Debate, Room 482, Woman's Own, Stamford Street, London SE1 9LS.

deprived of their childhood. Those who 'blur the boundary' between childhood and adulthood 'may be cheating children of childhood itself,' wrote Mary Whitehouse. 'In failing to treasure our children's childhood we are destroying not only their future but our own. We are like lemmings. We've got a death wish on us.' In the games played with the image, the 'joy and guileless innocence' Mary Whitehouse identified as the centre of childhood are maintained at considerable expense. Crises that force us to define it anew persist in rising to the surface of public consciousness. The media are forced to negotiate accounts of children who have sex, children who are wage-earners, children who don military uniform and fight in wars.

Yet the public discourse of which imagery plays so important a part strives to produce a childhood which, as well as being different from adulthood, is its obverse, a depository for many precious qualities adulthood needs but cannot tolerate as part of itself. The dichotomy child/adult is linked to other dichotomies which dominate our thought: nature/culture, primitiveness/civilisation, emotion/reason. In each pair the dominant term seeks to understand and control the subordinate, keeping it separate but using it for its own enrichment. From the engaging innocents in the baby books to the clued-up kids of contemporary advertising, behind pictures of children lies the desire to use childhood to secure the status of adulthood – often at the expense of children themselves.

The presence of a child – with its potential for blurring boundaries and confusing meanings – upsets an adult search for stability. Pictures remind us that childhood is never fully left behind, but also that our inner childhood is nothing like these delightful images. To quieten the anxiety, the image continues to be smoothed over and beautified. For all its modernisation, the nostalgic imagery of childhood refers overwhelmingly to a harmonious and comfortable world before industrial civilisation, when plenty did not depend on work or wealth. A rural idyll is pictured on milk cartons, bread wrappers, supermarket labels, advertisements for foodstuffs, and in high-gloss magazines about country living. There is a domesticated nature of gardens, wheatfields and pasture, a nature which provides for the needs of culture, where civilisation is firmly in control. Imagery made possible by the most highly developed technology re-creates pre-industrial, pre-technological values, scarring over the wounds. As coal mines are grassed over, factories are turned into art galleries and slums into garden centres, the image of childhood returns us to a fantasised pre-industrial childhood. Children are depicted in a countryside unpolluted by agri-business or nuclear fallout, cultivated by medieval means and inhabited by friendly little animals. Their saucer eyes link past and future, and they appear as a precious treasure in a corrupt world. In the constant renewal of childhood, the lost harmonious past can remain forever present and promise a future in which innocence is regained. In a world dominated by commercial imagery, a child can be shown standing outside commerce; in a world of rapid change, a child can be shown as unchanging; in a world of social and political conflict, a child is untainted. Children are for all time, forever new but always the same.

But ambivalence is always there. Cuteness itself is an acceptable play on the coexistence of innocence and knowledge, and the pictures which cause the greatest stir are the ones where the confusion becomes explicit – where girl children wear make-up and pose like adults, and it is difficult to distinguish play-acting from precociousness. In the search for the special qualities of childhood, it is the fragility of those qualities that we find so nervously attractive. Advertisements, sparing no expense to achieve the perfect picture, explore these elusive qualities. Newspapers make space for the 'most heart-warming pictures'.

Children who are poor, children from the Third World, children who are sick, harmed or disabled pose problems for the imagery, yet are necessary to it. Their experience means that they cannot be the bearers of joy and guileless innocence, yet their weakness is an essential part of childhood. They are extreme exemplars of children's dependent status. They stand as a warning to children who dare to resist their childish position.

Like childhood, photography claims innocence and authenticity. The more technologically perfect the picture, the more its mediating action is concealed. Kodak offers its customers 'real point and shoot simplicity . . . as easy as putting one foot in front of the other', and an important set of pictures of children appears in advertisements for family cameras. These are public pictures which train their viewers in the modes of private imagery. With their help, amateur snapshooters learn how to state and record those precious moments of family life. In the words of a Nikon advertisement, we 'make today's moments tomorrow's memories'. The instantly perfect, highly polished surface of the snapshot seems to offer a completed account, enabling us to relive the past relieved of its daily burdens. 'Your pictures will be judged by the amount of smile you manage to induce,' wrote Bernard Fearnley in his professional handbook *Child Photography*. He explained that photographers of children fall into two categories: 'They are either "stalkers" attempting to remain unnoticed by the child, or they are "directors" starting with a preconceived idea and exercising control over every detail of lighting, setting and handling of the child.' Directors must gain the confidence of the child subject by a knowledge of psychology, and a little duplicity is not out of place.

Parents follow the lead of the professionals and direct their children to produce smiles suitable for the family album, or silently follow them, camera in hand – assuming the right to spy on them in their most secret moments. Our gaze puts children in their place, conforms their image to expected patterns. Our look is a dual one of power and pleasure: the power which comes from knowledge of the subject, the pleasure of the beauty and seductiveness of childhood. Subject to our gaze, children must accept that power and grant us our pleasure – those who are defined do not have the right to look back and define in their turn. Instead it is *the picture* that looks back, placing the viewer in relation to its address.

Children – and especially girl children – must learn to present themselves *as* an image. They must learn a special sort of exhibitionism and reproduce in themselves the charming qualities adults long to see. They may recognise the pleasure that childhood provides for adults but must not reveal that knowledge, observing adult behaviour only secretly. Open refusal to co-operate invites punishment and a forced return to childishness in tears and humiliation. The imagery of children/childhood is part of an elaborate drama. The child models who people advertisements are experts in their role, yet they are treading on delicate ground. When children *invite* the adult gaze, when their beauty is no longer self-absorbed, when they deliberately put themselves on display, the result is a loss of innocence and childishness itself. While they engage in a tactful

amateur photographer

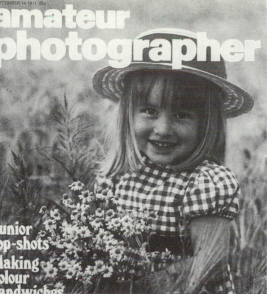

unior
op-shots

aking
olour
andwiches

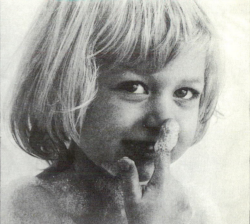

With the new Kodak pocket A-1 camera, it's as easy as utting one foot in front of the other.

Now you can take pictures of the family growing up, with a camera of your own.
The Kodak pocket A-1 camera.
All you do is drop in the film, aim and press the button. It's as simple as that.
No knobs to twiddle. Or dials to set.
Outside, or indoors with flash, you can take beautiful colour pictures that when printed, are almost twice the size of the camera itself.
And for about £12.50 it comes with a wrist-strap, carrying case, a 110 'Kodacolor' II film cartridge and a 3-year warranty.
So you really can't put a foot wrong, can you?

Kodak **Keep it with Kodak**

masquerade for the benefit of those who aim to control and enjoy them, the children in the advertisements and the family snaps continue to pose the question: who has the right to look, and under what circumstances?

Portraits of children, framed and presented for their beauty and charm, are, like the pin-up, part of the repertoire of the popular press. Their expressiveness invites our expressiveness. They are a signal for a release of emotions. When children accompany adults in a picture, it is they who may express what Roland Barthes called 'euphoric values'. The child in the picture opens a door to a libidinous existence, a life without constraints, a life of possibilities now forbidden. But together with ecstatic fulfilment comes the threat of total disruption. Childhood poses a challenge to the hard-won stability of adult civilisation. As the image of a child promises a richer world, in the same moment it threatens the security of the world we have.

Children introduce disorder and pollution into everyday life, and this theme runs alongside the idyllic beauty of childhood. The bodies of young children are leaky; they do not respect established boundaries: they wet the bed, spew up their food, have no respect for tidy kitchens or hoovered carpets. As they become older they roll in mud, cover themselves in paint, and bloody their hands and knees in falls and fights. Despite the recent – tentative – appearance of the caring father, it remains the role of the mother, as she appears in advertisements for soap powder and washing machines, to whisk away soiled clothing, wrap the little bodies in bath foam and fluffy towels, remove pollutants and restore cleanliness. But the cleansing rituals associated with childcare can go only so far; the child retains a potential for total disruption. Another set of public narratives speaks of little monsters, threatening their parents, refusing to listen and calling for extremes of restraint and control. Consumer imagery of mini-gangsters and precocious temptresses plays with the danger, taunting it, keeping it at bay. But when the paradoxes of the 'natural' are replaced by the paradoxes of civilisation, when children move beyond constraint and surveillance and run together in the urban streets, the fear is genuine. This is where we find the terrifying image of youth, of children alone together beyond the reach of family or school, sufficient in each other's company, acting out a mythological conflict between spontaneity and control.

In posing questions about rationality and order, the image searches the margins of humanity itself. Children are said to be like animals, close to madness or the supernatural. By drawing attention to the boundary between the natural and the human, the presence of a child throws the very status of civilisation into question. With such fears in mind, every sort of restraint against children becomes legitimate. Their resistance is seen as 'naughtiness'. Their rights to independent action or thought are almost non-existent, depending on the whim of parents or carers. And children remain the objects of imagery, almost never its makers. Their voices are missing, defined as incapable of meaningful expression. They should be seen but not heard. Like all groups without power they suffer the indignity of being unable to present themselves as they would want to be seen – or, indeed, of even considering how they might want to be seen. They are not in a position to manufacture a public image for themselves and have no control over the image others make of them. In consequence, as they become adults, individuals have only impoverished ways of expressing their own remembered childhoods.

The harsh dichotomies of the image intensify the sense of loss in the adult concept of childhood, yet we all feel we have something of Peter Pan in us. Our own childhood, buried deep in memory and only partially recaptured in present experience, plays against relationships with present-day children. Adults demand from children something they can never give, for we are seeking our own past as much as their present. Engaging pictures of children are dealing with that gap. If our childhood is all but lost, childhood itself can be protected, hedged around with prohibitions, held firm by those who hold it in trust for the moment. Constructed versions of childhood attempt to bring our own elusive childhoods into line. Pictures of children provide the grounds for a dialogue between our past and our present. They problematise any easy reference to memory and enforce a link between our psychic and our social continuity.

In its social aspect, the image of childhood poses the problem of generations, of continuity and renewal. Children are expected to mature into the established patriarchal order, yet they stand as a threat to that order. Their challenge may be interpreted as an instability which must be repressed in the interests of civilisation or as a challenge in the name of a better society. Paul Goodman, whose *Growing up Absurd* was first published in 1956, had argued the case for 'childlike' values to permeate and improve society. Then children would retain their 'right to wildness' and relations between children and adults would evolve that would not be based on coercion and domination.

But any right is meaningless if it is merely expressed by adults on behalf of children. The point when the popular concept of childhood breaks down is when it runs up against children's own expression. This is not because children's expressions have special qualities which differ from those of adults, but because they come from a radically different perspective with very little outlet in contemporary media. Without any input from children themselves, childhood can only remain an impossible concept, always mediated by adulthood, its guileless innocence searched for but never found. However well they learn to play the part, actual children can never fulfil such a fantasy.

The constructed category of childhood meets limits of a different sort when the discourse around childhood is extended to include forbidden areas like work, sex and war, when children are performing a decisively non-childish role. The imagery that speaks of childhood sexuality is prolific and fraught with contradictions. The imagery that deals with child labour and children at war is less frequent and tends to be confined to campaigns to protect children from these inappropriate activities. As Judith Ennew makes clear in her book *The Sexual Exploitation of Children*, children are regularly present in all these areas, in Britain as well as in less privileged parts of the world. But their presence has no recognised social validity, and is largely invisible.

An imagery that reaches for an abstract concept of childhood is, nevertheless, placed within specific historical moments and itself contributes to political and social conflict. The last twenty years

began with utopian visions of children's liberation and ended with major domestic scandals over child sexual abuse, shocking reports of children's starvation across the continent of Africa and increasing child poverty throughout the world. Nonetheless, in Britain, the most fertile source of public imagery of children is produced as a necessary part of a consumer-based economy. In this blissful world of plenty, pictures of children are commodities, and they promote other commodities, enhancing their desirability. But while the consumer image becomes ever more euphoric, in stark contrast, the image of a child suffering from harsh conditions or damaged at the hands of adults has pushed more and more into public consciousness. We have become accustomed to pictures of children sleeping rough in British cities, publicity which highlights drug abuse amongst children, and the victims of sexual abuse, who can be shown only in shadow, or with their backs to the camera. In major disasters across the world, caused by war, famine and the human exploitation of resources, children are the first to suffer, and pictures of emaciated children close to death have become the symbols through which the magnitude of those disasters have penetrated Western media.

In 1989 the United Nations General Assembly finally adopted a Convention on the Rights of the Child after more than thirty years of negotiation. Such slow progress does not bode well for the children of the future. But when their voices are finally heard, adults' definitions, too, will of necessity be less rigid. They may be replaced not by other definitions but by an approach that is sensitive to the ever-shifting perspectives of meaning. In such a context we might see the evolution of an imagery of childhood which reaches beyond an adult attempt to dominate and define.

1

There's no such thing as a baby . . .

I once risked the remark 'there's no such thing as a baby', meaning that if you set out to describe a baby you are describing *a baby and someone*. A baby cannot exist alone but is essentially part of a relationship.

D.W. Winnicott

Floating calmly at the centre of one of the most acrimonious disputes of the decade, the image of the fetus stands for perfect peace and security. As technology has pushed the possibility of survival to earlier and earlier moments in pregnancy, the revelation of sentient and coherent life well before birth has transformed the public concept of the beginnings of childhood. The contest around the meaning of childhood begins at that indeterminate point and, as with every other context in the interweaving narratives, the status of children always carries implications for those who surround them, and most of all for the woman who bears them. The rights of the fetus – the unborn child – have become a rallying cry for those who would define women primarily as mothers. But the fury is only obliquely reflected in the image. The fetus, and sometimes the very young baby too, enter available imagery as symbols of harmony and calm. Life in the womb is shown, improbably, as a time of total satisfaction, foreshadowing a utopian future. The child is surrounded by a supernatural aura or becomes a water baby, revelling in nakedness and fluidity.

The fantasy is broken by the violent imagery of birth. Presentations of birth work hard to calm the unwelcome disruption, but

FOR NINE MONTHS HE GETS EVERYTHING HE NEEDS FROM ONE PLACE.

WHY CHANGE THE HABIT OF A LIFETIME?

For nine months he's got it all worked out. Food, clothes, furnishings and transport all under one convenient roof. Why should it be any different when he's born?

At Childrens World he can get everything he needs. Except now it's made by Boots, Pampers, Silver Cross, Tomy and us.

We've even made a few improvements on his original; free car parks, hairdressers and special mother and baby changing rooms. It should all make moving home less of an upheaval.

EVERYTHING IN THE WORLD FOR CHILDREN

Childrens World is open 10am to 8pm on weekdays, 9am to 6pm on Saturdays. Call 081-200 0200 for details of your nearest store. Childrens World is part of the Boots Group.

pictures of children at the beginning of their separate existence display and arouse extreme emotions. The face of the newborn crumples and distorts. Its body is streaked with blood and messy substances. The surroundings are medical – although more recently hints of white tiles and metal instruments have been replaced with warm colours and flowery curtains. A specialist of some kind, doctor or midwife, is reassuringly in command. When the photographer Grace Robertson shot a sequence of pictures documenting the experience of birth for the news magazine *Picture Post* in 1956, the magazine refused to print them on the grounds that they would be too upsetting for their readers. But attitudes change, and twenty years later, in 1976, *Parents* magazine published a second-by-second sequence as the bloodstained head of the baby emerged. These pictures showed sex organs and pubic hair, but the public remained protected from the mother's agonised effort. In the final picture she lies comfortably against the pillows as the midwife hands the infant to her.

The medical context, the clinical observation, the empiricism and rational sequencing of a series of pictures like this, serve to demythologise and normalise the moment of childbirth for its participants.

Parents

April 1976

Childbirth

Second-by-second colour photographs of the birth of this baby—a perfectly normal delivery. But what happens when babies take up unusual positions inside the mother? See Page 20

Pregnancy

Preparing yourself psychologically for childbirth can be as helpful as physical health. We tell you how on Page 8

Holidays

How to make sure your family holiday goes with a swing, and that children stay happy on even the longest journey. Page 63

Supertoy

This may not look like one of the most creative toys ever invented—but we think it is. For details, see Page 33

A-Z

SPECIAL: Part 1 of all you need to know about children's illnesses—The A-Z of Child Health. Page 43

Marriage

Are you really fulfilled in your relationship? We say there's hardly a marriage in which sexual relations can't be improved. Read about it on Page 75

Fathers

How do fathers cope with family chores? We took two to a supermarket and asked them to do the shopping. Find out how they rated on Page 17

Parents 3

Second by second, these photographs show in astonishing detail the decisive phase of childbirth — the emergence of the baby's head. The mother of the baby whose birth you are witnessing has been waiting six hours for delivery to begin. Now, only a few minutes more, and her child will be born . . .

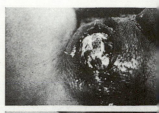

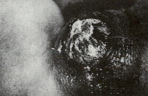

During the fourth series of contractions, the head begins to show through

Parents 23

24

This has remained the aim of the burgeoning magazines for the young mother market – quite a different audience from the one which followed the political commentary and black-and-white photo-reports in *Picture Post*. *Picture Post* was the pioneer of illustrated magazines, but the twenty years which separated the two saw the coming of full-colour printing, the launch of the Sunday colour supplements which balanced photojournalism with increasingly sophisticated advertising and, most recently, the proliferation of consumer magazines precisely targeted at specific audiences. Indeed, the biggest change in the imagery of babyhood over the last two decades has been the shift from pictures produced in the context of welfare and professional advice to pictures produced in the context of advertising and marketing. By the late 1980s there were nine paid-for baby magazines, most printed in lush colours on quality paper. Giving birth and caring for a baby at the end of the twentieth century has become a purchasing, consumer-based activity. Advertisers advise on babycare, the advice columns review products, and pictures of happy, healthy babies illustrate both. At the same time these pages have become the contemporary forum for gossip and the exchange of experience – particularly of childbirth stories. *Parents*

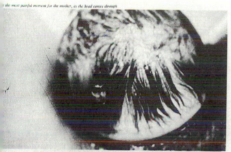

the most painful moment for the mother, as the head comes through

The baby is born, the cord cut. The mother sees a tiny, wet, screaming bundle of life—her baby

time difference between the first and last pictures you here is just four seconds. The back of the head shows

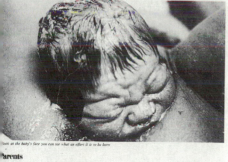

look at the baby's face you can see what an effort it is to be born

anticipated, the normal onset of labour is awaited. Some obstetricians tend to start labour one or two weeks before full term, particularly if the neck of the womb (the cervix) seems ready and "ripe", as it may be slightly easier for the breech baby to come out if it is a little smaller.

Labour with a breech baby is usually normal but it must take place in a hospital. Sometimes it may be a little slower because the bottom does not fit the lower part of the womb as snugly as the head, and may therefore be less effective in pushing open the cervix. A substance called syntocinon can then be given by a drip into a vein to strengthen the action of the womb and avoid an overlong labour. The delivery must be performed by a doctor, although he interferes as little as possible, giving a little help here and there, and leaving most of it up to the mother. After some local anaesthetic has been given (or an epidural anaesthetic), a small cut (an episiotomy) is made to enlarge the vaginal outlet and to help the delivery of the baby. Finally, as the head comes last, forceps are gently applied to protect its passage backwards through the pelvis.

When the baby is lying in the usual manner with the head down, it is most favourable if the back of its head points forwards because the smallest diameters of the head then pass through the pelvis. Quite frequently, however, especially in first pregnancies, the back of the

After the pain and excitement: the mother smiles, the midwife is happy; the baby risks its first sidelong glance at the world

head points towards the mother's back and the baby looks upwards. In these circumstances, the diameters of the head passing down the birth canal are slightly larger.

This often causes the baby's head to be high before labour commences, creates more work for the womb, and means that labour may take somewhat longer. During the course of labour, the head usually turns into the normal position, but sometimes it gets stuck half-way, the back of the head pointing sideways. The delivery then has to be assisted by a doctor, either using special forceps with which he can rotate the head to the normal position, or by applying a suction cup to the baby's head and connecting it to a vacuum. Modern methods of pain relief are very effective for these procedures and the mother need not fear them.

Much more rarely, the baby's forehead or face comes first, or it may be lying transversely or obliquely in the womb. Here, a caesarean section is often necessary, but provided these conditions are recognised in time, and the mother is in hospital, both she and her baby will be safe ●

The Nuclear War Game
ADAM SUDDABY

has a feature called 'Delivery Notes'; *Mother and Baby* invites 'your favourite birth stories' and features compare hospitals and birth styles – now an aid to consumer choice. But the tone is intimate and informal, and pictures are often those sent in by readers. They tend to show the moment after the birth when the baby rests comfortably on the mother's body. A potential image of crisis is transformed into an image of calm, recaptured by the desire for a pacified, domestic regime.

Any hint that baby and mother are not always in harmony is kept well under control. In his famous *Birth Without Violence*, Frédérick Leboyer used photographs to demonstrate the baby's traumatic experience of birth. The agonised face of the newborn infant is ignored by the celebrating adults, as the doctor holds the baby upside down like a fisherman's catch. Leboyer's work was influential in the move to make childbirth techniques gentler and less technological, but the tortured image retained its power. Many years later it was used by the peace movement to express the antithesis of the beatific fetus, the ultimate in human distress, the crumpled face and helpless arms of the baby forming the mushroom cloud of a nuclear explosion. Leboyer himself compared the face of the baby who had experienced a peaceful birth to the serene face of the buddha. Though the turbulence of birth is rarely glimpsed in the iconography of babyhood, the possibility of distress continues to hover darkly in the background.

Yet the available imagery gives an overwhelming impression of harmony. A new baby, especially a famous one, makes its first public appearance in the arms of the woman who bore it and now presents it to the world. Midwives, doctors and professional helpers are no longer needed. The faces of woman and baby can both be shown in mutual satisfaction. Mothers of the 1970s took up the traditional posture, cradling the infant in their arms. Mothers of the 1980s are more likely to turn to the camera, displaying the little creature, sometimes in joyful nakedness. But we must never forget that we are looking at imagery at work. Although there is a baby at the centre of these presentations, the image is working on the meaning of 'woman', ensuring a smooth transformation into 'mother'. Whoever she is – famous or unknown, glamorous model or a reader who has sent her picture to the editor – many consequences flow from her redefinition.

In a more intimate image, now exemplified by anonymous mothers, the crook of the woman's arm, instead of serving to display the baby to the gaze on the onlookers, draws the child inwards, supporting it in the act of suckling. The image is shaped by the curve of her arm and the downward tilt of her head. It is sometimes emphasised by oval framing. Her gaze is totally concentrated on the

PROTECT YOUR BABY

What parents should know about immunisation of children early in life

feeding

THE NATURAL CHOICE

Whenever possible babies should be breast fed – there is no better food for young babies. Breast feeding is a natural process and helps ensure a strong physical as well as emotional bond between you and your baby. Your own milk contains all the goodness your baby needs, free of contamination and at exactly the right temperature.

The choice is yours, and if for any reason you are unable to breast feed, don't feel guilty but consult your health professionals on the right way to feed your baby – they will be pleased to help you. Mothercare offer a breast pump and a wide range of products to complement natural feeding.

baby. Here is an exclusive couple, unaware that they are the objects of our contemplation. No background or surroundings are needed as the image explores the closeness of the relationship. At the centre of such pictures is that highly charged object, a woman's breast. Here it is clearly defined as a mother's breast, for in our culture she, and only she, has the privilege and duty to offer it to her child. Such pictures appear in exemplary contexts – books of advice for new mothers, advertisements, collections of photography as art. They forge an iron link between woman and child, for we cannot fail to see the woman as mother of the baby and the baby as child of the woman. These exemplary women are universalised into examples of motherhood itself as the relationship is confirmed by their intimate physical contact and held by their mutual gaze.

An advertisement from 1991 and a medical expert from 1981 are amongst many others who emphasise the point: 'A mother and her baby. Two people who, for the next few years of their lives, will be inseparable. Emotionally. Physically.' . . . 'You will find yourself completely preoccupied by him. You and your baby are not yet wholly separate people, and in some ways you never will be.' The curved logo of the National Childbirth Trust continues to fuse the couple into one.

The baby changes the nature of the woman whose arms encircle it. In her study of the myth and cult of the Virgin Mary, *Alone of All Her Sex*, Marina Warner describes the fourteenth-century transformation of Mary from a transcendent queen into the ideal of feminine humility and submission, brought about when she was seen above all as a mother: 'In motherhood Mary was glorified and through her position before her child became more glorious for her humility.' Outside the Roman Catholic Church, thousands who would otherwise take no part in the cult of Mary as Madonna circulate her image. Mother and baby are placed somewhere beyond the everyday world, sanctified with a halo, associated with the solemn, if childlike, aspects of Christmas and the hushed intensity of the art gallery. The holiness of the couple is secured by their freedom from worldliness and sexuality. They have aesthetic as well as exemplary value. Thus the private relationship has a public dimension which places it firmly in this history of Culture, and its social form is all the harder to shift. Contemporary pictures of active mothers and babies refusing to be shaped by the curve of the image can be read as a resistance to the pull of these powerful pressures.

While such imagery seeks to limit the possible meanings of 'woman' to those associated with 'mother', at the same time it encourages an infinite expansion of the possible meanings of 'baby'. When you hold a baby 'you've got the whole world in your hands', warns an advertisement for Infocare bath products. The baby represents the potential of all humanity. In contemporary baby magazines the child is as likely to be a 'she' as a 'he', but until very recently writers have found it difficult to reconcile such universality with the feminine pronoun. 'It is tedious to put "he and she" and it also saves confusion when "she" is the mother', the BMA told their readers tetchily in 1976. In a 1991 pamphlet the Child Accident Prevention Trust put the explanation at its starkest: 'This booklet refers to all babies as "he" or "him" to make for easier reading.'

This universal 'he' who makes for easier reading and must be defined in antithesis to 'she', the mother, is not the 'he' of a potent and active masculinity but a more generalised 'he', a godlike manifestation of humanity itself who, merely by existing, can command service and nurture from 'she'. At this point 'she' seems little more than an encircling and protecting environment, Mother Nature, the providing earth.

The transformation of woman into nurturing mother depends on the transformation of her breast. Pictures of breastfeeding mothers show a three-point relationship – not just between woman and baby but between woman, baby and breast. That part of women's bodies which is surrounded by taboos and fascinations must here be seen as chaste and desexualised. The breast poses a problem for the image, just as it poses a practical problem for women who want to feed their babies on a day trip or a shopping expedition. We are assured, however, that this breast is quite different from the provocative breasts of the topless sunbathers, the joke-shop falsies or the top shelf at the local newsagent's. Unlike the arrogant breasts on Page Three, these visible breasts should not be seen as an assertive element of female display. Indeed, 'as she prepares to feed him . . . her breasts change in appearance in a subtle and beautiful way', the BMA informed new mothers. In order to differentiate a mother's breast from a woman's breast, the imagery must struggle to retain 'mother' as an asexual category, despite – and because of – the exposure of her breast. The struggle centres on her visible contact with the baby. Although writers such as Sheila Kitzinger have discussed the potentially sexual experience of breastfeeding, the visible touch between this 'he' and 'she' must repress the sexual implications of that antithesis. The baby is presented as the object of 'her' love and concern, but the breast is the object of 'his' desire. Their relationship is not reciprocal. Just as in some forms of psychoanalytic discourse the breast appears as a separate entity with which the baby builds a relationship before becoming aware of the mother as an individual, this image, too, while seeking to present the satisfaction of the nursing couple, can eliminate the woman altogether.

The picture may be cropped, so that her face is eliminated from the frame and her ambivalent emotions are not visible. When her face is included, her joy and delight appear as a reflection of his joy and delight. Although the similarity between mother and lover is disguised by an array of taboos and prohibitions, it emerges in the sense of nervous impropriety behind a headline like 'How was I to know it was not my baby at my breast?' and the saucy joke behind the 1991 advertisement for Triumph nursing bras: 'There are times when you can allow the man in your life to choose your bra.' The 1984 advertisement for Cow and Gate baby foods, which shockingly showed the breast only as food – 'May we suggest the liver and bacon to follow?' – won advertising industry awards for both effectiveness and creativity. In these ways the sensuous touching between lips and breast is carefully negotiated. The baby is allowed full flow of 'his' emotions, but the mother must temper hers in the knowledge of her responsibility and service. Viewers of these presentations must appreciate the satisfactions experienced by the baby and disavow their own erotic response.

The bottle enters the popular imagery of babyhood very much as second best, usually in advertisements for formula baby food. Its intrusive nipple accompanies the 'honest' admission that 'breast is best' and offers itself as a humble but adequate substitute. As breastfeeding declined in Britain throughout the 1980s, campaigners from organisations like Baby Milk Action pointed to pressure from the baby milk manufacturers and to the 'glossy little brochures

featuring smiling babies and baby milk brands which are placed on maternity ward bedside tables'. Such promotion is specifically forbidden under the World Health Organisation code established in 1981 after the exposure of methods used by Nestlé to sell formula baby milk to mothers in poorer parts of the Third World. Although the Conservative government signed the WHO code, national standards for Britain were devised by the industry's lobby, the Food Manufacturers' Federation, who used the opportunity to encourage advertising to health workers and new mothers. In 1989 the *Health Visitor Journal* rejected an advertisement for Farley's Ostermilk which showed two tins placed in the two cups of a bra because, they said, it associated the formula too closely with breast milk. Throughout this debate, the breast remains a central value, the one secure link between mother and baby.

The rival claims of breast milk and formula are one aspect of the tension between the 'natural' and the 'scientific' in advice to mothers and its attendant imagery. 'It is a gift bestowed by nature. That special something which bonds mother and baby. That magic touch that brings comfort to the distressed child.' So wrote Edward Vale in the *Daily Mirror* on the occasion of Prince William's christening in August 1982. He was addressing the *Mirror*'s two million readers of assorted ages and sexes. At about the same time, 'a professor of obstetrics and gynaecology' addressed the much more specific audience of women who were about to become mothers in another advice leaflet. 'Having a baby is a recurring miracle and still the biggest

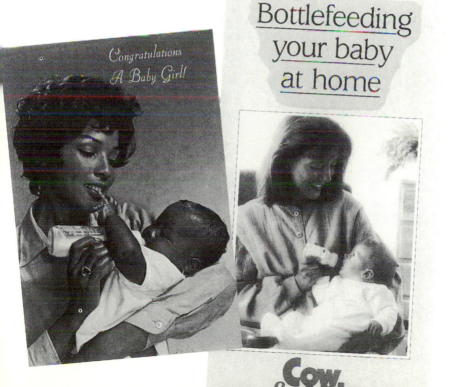

event in a woman's life,' he reassured them. 'Don't worry if you don't feel a great surge of mother love. This unique bond between mother and child takes a little time to develop.' Both writers managed to hold together references to the supernatural – 'that magic touch' . . . 'a recurring miracle' – with the natural – 'a gift bestowed by nature' – and with science. A 'bond' will develop inexorably, and a professor may identify and explain it.

The emphasis on the natural regularly leads writers into the paradox of advising against advice, quoting Benjamin Spock's famous dictum: 'You know more than you think you do'. When child development expert Martin Richards said in a 1990 interview: 'I liked the idea of writing directly to parents and encouraging them to reject the compendiums of "expert" advice', he was echoing many others from D.W. Winnicott in the 1940s to Penelope Leach, who wrote in the mid 1970s: 'Although this is a book, it will not suggest you do things "by the book".' Even so, for most professional advisers it is better to do things by the book than to pay attention to the other forms of distraction they list. The spoken word is always suspect, particularly when it is spoken by the untrained or by mothers,

Does a baby natur

A baby is not born with the ability to feel love as adults do. He is born with only the basic needs and wants . . .

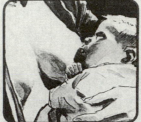

. . . for food, warmth, comfort. When these needs are satisfied, he feels good, as he's no longer unsatisfied.

If every time the needs arise, they are dealt with at once by same person, soon the baby begins to learn to . . .

Does a mother n

Some mothers do feel love for a newborn baby. But most need to "fall in love" just as the baby does.

She is "triggered" to respond to his suckling with physical pleasure. His cry fills her breasts with milk . . .

. . . and the satisfaction feedin gives him makes him smile, which provides further pleasu for her . . .

neighbours or friends from an older generation. Wisdom no longer resides in the accumulated knowledge of the past, but in the future enlightenment and scientific advance. 'Instinct' offers the main guidance, the guidance of nature, but since instinct is not immediately accessible, it must be trained, mediated by science and expert knowledge. Informal accounts and the experience of previous generations stand awkwardly outside these accepted forms.

When new mothers feel that nature has failed them, the experts reassure them by referring them to science. Penelope Leach describes how the bond between mother and child will develop: 'His responses create a self-sustaining circle, his smiles leading to your smiles and yours to more from him.' A cartoon strip from a Health Education Council leaflet sets out in diagrammatic form how the key images of mothers and babies are achieved as a sequence of looks and responses is exchanged between the pair, each working to 'trigger' the other. Among the frames we find the classic Madonna-and-baby couple, the suckling baby engrossed in the breast and the laughing, responsive baby face.

ve his Mother?

ociate his comfort with rson. Being with that means feeling good : e means feeling bad.

And so he "falls in love" with the person, whoever it may be, who inhabits the very centre of his whole world.

Whether it is his biological mother, or a foster or adopting mother, a man or a woman, makes no difference.

love her Baby?

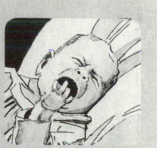

so they "trigger" each fall in love at the same

But the process can be spoiled if the baby isn't given to his mother enough just after birth. Or if she

is too worried about money, or other troubles she may be unable to respond to him.

It is this last image that is most actively sought by newspapers, baby magazines and, increasingly, advertisers for products from perfume to motorcars. As the diagram sequence so graphically illustrates, this is the face of the baby from the point of view of the devoted mother, the baby face she longs to see, whch secures a bond that is magic, natural and amenable to scientific explanation. So local papers run their 'beautiful baby' competitions, advertising agencies leaf through casting catalogues of model babies, and baby magazines vie with each other for the most gorgeous baby face for their covers. Research from an American journal, *Animal Behaviour*, was reported with diagrams in the British press in 1977. It sought to demonstrate that only some babies have faces which fulfil the criteria for bonding, with dire consequences for those who do not conform: 'The preference is instinctive, not social.' Small chins and wide eyes make a more effective 'trigger' for mother love: 'We ought to consider the possibility that if their baby has a face that doesn't trigger the benevolent instinct, the brutal behaviour of their parents (that is, child-batterers) would then be cruel and appalling, but in the precise sense of the word, natural.'

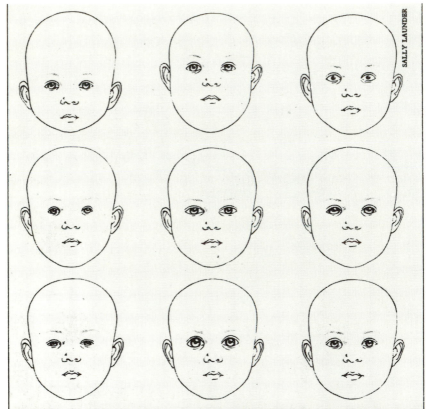

American ethologists (scientists who study behaviour) have researched the most attractive facial characteristics in infants. Wide eyes and small chins rate highly

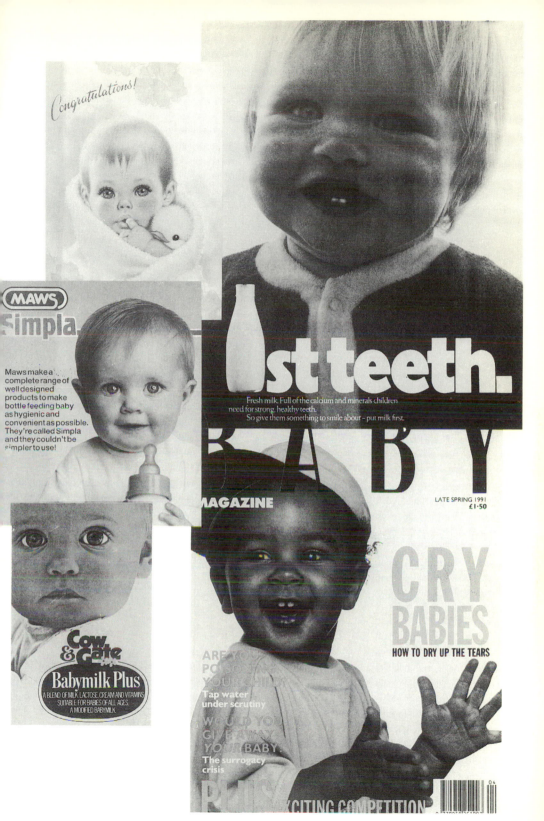

Congratulations!

MAWS
Simpla

Maws make a complete range of well designed products to make bottle feeding baby as hygienic and convenient as possible. They're called Simpla and they couldn't be simpler to use!

Cow & Gate
Babymilk Plus
A BLEND OF MILK, LACTOSE, CREAM AND VITAMINS SUITABLE FOR BABIES OF ALL AGES. A MODIFIED BABYMILK.

1st teeth.
Fresh milk. Full of the calcium and minerals children need for strong, healthy teeth.
So give them something to smile about – put milk first.

BABY
MAGAZINE
LATE SPRING 1991
£1·50

CRY
BABIES
HOW TO DRY UP THE TEARS

ARE YOUR
POTS IN
YOUR SINK
Tap water under scrutiny

WOULD YOU
GIVE AWAY
YOUR BABY
The surrogacy crisis

PLUS
EXCITING COMPETITION

37

The fear that without the 'trigger' to secure the 'bond' – natural yet confirmed by science – women may escape the duties of motherhood was reiterated by the hospital which provided photographs of babies in intensive care for their mothers to keep with them, to assist the bonding process: 'If the bond is loosened, a demanding baby can be too much for a mother to tolerate.' Thus the faces which gurgle at mothers from Junior Disprol packets, Fisher Price advertisements and the magazine shelves at W.H. Smith are the faces of *beautiful* babies, their beauty judged by their rounded symmetrical faces, their wide sparkling eyes and their appealing expressions. 'Because the agency insists that the babies in the ads have to be just right, casting is a tricky business,' wrote Gail Kemp in *Campaign* of the Cow and Gate advertisements. The eyes are usually blue and the faces are the softest of pinks. Only towards the end of the 1980s have Black babies begun to appear in advertising and in the editorial pages. *Baby Magazine* is the only one to have developed a thoroughly multiethnic approach, using Black babies on its covers and running a regular feature on babies around the world.

The trigger of maternal love can also trigger maternal purchases. The expansion of the baby magazine market came in the late 1980s, with five new launches and two relaunches, at a time when parents were having fewer children, spending more on each of them, and 'bringing up babies was chic'. By 1990 the 'fashion' for voguish parenthood meant that babies were considered suitable triggers for a wide range of products, for men as well as women, and concern was expressed that the practice was, in itself, an exploitation, an unfair arousal of parental emotion. *Campaign* invited comments from its readers. The not-so-serious replies it received were summed up by the 'baby' who wrote: 'Some people are simply jealous of our success and glamorous lifestyles.'

The cover-baby smiles the delighted smile that mothers long to see, but this perfect picture is difficult to achieve – even for advertisers with plenty of resources and cash to spend. It may all too easily be spoiled. Truby King, the austere mentor of an earlier generation of childcare experts, was obsessed with the possibility of 'spoiling'. 'Any baby can easily be spoiled and made a cross, fretful and exacting little tyrant,' he wrote in 1912. Pictures of babies in their fretful and tyrannical moods are far less frequently seen, and are never allowed to dominate a page. A baby may bring disruption so awful that it is best dealt with by resorting to comedy. The situation is made light of and things are soon put right. The peaceful image may be restored either by one of innumerable branded products – Anebesol, Dinnifords, Johnson and Johnson nappy liners – or by the advice of experts. Even so, the imagery makes it clear that it remains the task of the mother to maintain harmony within the domestic

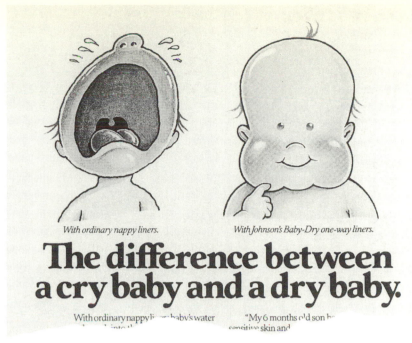

With ordinary nappy liners.

With Johnson's Baby-Dry one-way liners.

The difference between a cry baby and a dry baby.

With ordinary nappy li... baby's water

"My 6 months old son h...
sensitive skin and

setting. She may turn her gaze out of the frame towards the viewer, looking beyond the self-sufficiency of the nursing couple. Sometimes the baby in distress may also look beyond its mother, as if appealing for help. Yet the suggestion that the perfect couple of mother and child is incomplete is once more rapidly recuperated. Dissatisfaction is shown only so that satisfaction may be restored. When Mum needs help, when she lacks the specialised expertise and equipment, when 'a cuddle isn't enough', another character, although not always a visible one, must help restore order. In consumer imagery the work is done by the product. In advice literature the doctor, nurse or health visitor puts in a helpful appearance.

Asilone for Infants
new arrival in the Asilone family.

To the trusted Asilone range comes a suspension for infant
formulation with the gentle power to help mum quickly reduce ...
pains and regurgitation in even the youngest infant.
Asilone for Infants contains dimethicone + antacids, has ...
blackcurrant flavour and can easily be mixed with feeds.
She may wonder why we didn't introduce it before.

In the eczemas of childhood
No need to sacrifice
effectiveness for safety

Molivate

Molivate is an ideal corticosteroid for childhood eczemas - such as
atopic eczema - because it has been shown to be significantly
effective than hydro...

When the imagery is dominated by its welfare aspects – which include advertising for medicines, toiletries and other products concerned with health and hygiene – the clinical eye supervises the parental eye. Professional scrutiny sets standards as growth and development are measured, monitored and assessed. *'You and Your Baby* will help you because it is written by experts who will tell you what is normal and what is not', was the confident assertion which began a late-1970s BMA booklet. The normative regime of science enters the home, and the imagery, in the guise of an – often uniformed – professional. The baby never totally leaves the discursive space of medicine and welfare, where the observation and measurement of change are all-important. Today, when mothers are increasingly seen as customers rather than clients, the prolific imagery of the baby magazines provides a visual repertoire of child development, both as yardstick and as reassurance. Each expected change offers its own opportunities to the photographer. 'A general itinerary of his rapid journey from infancy and babyhood into childhood has been plotted by the Yale University Clinic of Child Development after close observation of thousands of children. Each of these stages of development provides valuable insights as to what to look for as photographic behaviour', wrote the editors of the Time-Life book *Photographing Children*.

Until recently, medical advisers appeared in advertisements and advice literature rather more frequently than fathers. But the days when new mothers were advised: 'Rather let the housework go than neglect your husband' have rapidly been giving way to fathers' demands to take part in the pleasures of parenting. *Practical Parenting* told new fathers: 'The birth of your baby can be one of the greatest highlights in your life.' Fathers of the late 1980s were seen feeding the baby and enjoying the sensuous pleasure of a small body against the skin. At least in the image, the father moved from his supportive background position to take centre stage with the baby. 'Alienated, self-absorbed manhood is becoming redundant as a marketing tool', declared John Hegarty of advertising agency Bartle, Bogle, Hegarty.

In the mid 1980s, *Mother* – the oldest of the baby magazines, which finally closed in 1990 – ran a regular column by 'role-reversing father' Stephen Lugg, pictured at his typewriter in his frilly apron. But the new image of fatherhood was a more sexy one. Advertisers identified a 'thirtysomething' culture, 'a slackening of the fierce ambitions that gripped the '80s', a more home-centred and relaxed approach, seeking pleasure with the children. It seemed that fathers were almost ousting mothers in their anxiety to be a mother-like parent, to play a non-masculine, caring role. When, in 1990, *The Times* announced its 'new baby' – its Saturday magazine – it was a man,

Growth.
Confidence.
Security.

Somehow the future never
quite takes care of itself.
Now and then it needs a little
help. The sort of help the Halifax
can give.
With the Halifax, saving is so simple.
You can choose
from five different schemes.
All offering the opportunity of
a consistently competitive return
with a high degree of security.
Get to know the
Halifax today.
Tomorrow will look
that much brighter.

HALIFAX
BUILDING SOCIETY
Member of the Building Societies Association

The biggest in the world

The Meek may Inherit
the Earth but Should they
Inherit your Debts?

You want to give her the world. A new
playpen today, a secondhand hatch-
back tomorrow. And why not, you can
borrow the money. But what if your
days were numbered? Would your
family be buried under your debts?

If you take out a loan with Mercantile
Credit, there's no need to worry.
Because if you die, we will partially
repay your outstanding balance, as
long as you were under the age of
60 when you signed the agreement.

Just fill in the coupon or call us
completely free of charge and we'll
send you an application form for
a loan from £400 to £15,000 with
life protection thrown in. It really is
the sensible way to borrow money.

The Times' new baby.

Starting this week The Times Saturday Review
will bring the weekend alive
with brilliant writers and dramatic colour.
It will involve our intelligent,
interesting readers in an intelligent,
interesting way. It will give advertisers the
precision of short copy dates,
magazine format and the most upmarket family
of readers of any newspaper.
The Saturday Review will deliver. The Times
has new bounce.

THE **TIMES**
Saturday Review
THE **PLACE**

naked from the waist up, who caressed the baby on its posters. In 1991 the Body Shop promoted a 'labour day pack' with stylish photographs in sculptural black and white. But the arms encircling the wriggling infant were unmistakably male. In this 'new age', neo-Romantic vision of birth, which positively celebrates the sensuality of the flesh, both men and women can share the pleasurable touch. In a range of presentations, babyhood has come to legitimise nakedness. The one medium where unclothed bodies and intertwined limbs have become a regular – if sometimes questioned – part of public imagery is the baby magazines.

But the practicalities of 1990s babycare include increasing numbers of working mothers and single parents. The mother of the 1990s may be a soldier leaving for the Gulf War, or a member of the target readership of *She*. At the magazine's relaunch in March 1990, *She* told its advertisers that a 'massive, growing, attractive and affluent market' is made up of mothers who 'juggle their lives', balancing committed motherhood with work and an active social life: 'You need the juggler and we've got her.' But one character is notably absent from this hedonistic claim that it is possible to have things all ways. We never see babies with nannies or childminders. We almost never see them in crèches. The non-professional childcare workers without whom mothers could not work, however hard they juggle, are virtually invisible. There seems to be no place for these important working women in the imagery of consumerism. Increasingly, those addressed are only those who are affluent and attractive to advertisers. Those delightfully smiling faces, appealingly naked bodies, and the romping, tumbling, wriggling, playful pictures which have made the imagery of babyhood richer than ever before, are presented within a narrowing social framework.

embassy wives weep for heroes left behind to face the wrath of Hussein's bully boys ★★TODAY Saturday August 25.

MUMS OFF TO BATTLE

FINAL EMBRACE: U.S. army medic Nollie Vallance kisses seven-week-old daughter Cheyenne goodbye

2
Superbrats in the charmed circle of home

When the father invades the imagery of babyhood, he may attempt to imitate the perfection of the nursing couple, but usually his arrival is more tentative – as an admiring and protective third party. His intervention in the picture, rather than imitating the mother–baby relationship, changes it, and a different kind of harmony settles on the image. The inward-turned oval becomes a sharper triangle, with the man at its peak. The group becomes a 'family'.

Popular imagery provides us with visual equivalents of the concept. Deeply troubled by such issues as one-parent families, adoption, mixed-race families and – as technology develops – by artificial insemination, *in vitro* fertilisation and – most shocking of all – surrogacy, which separates childbearing from motherhood, the traditional idea of 'family' has been challenged to the point where the concept itself must surely collapse. Yet the narrowest of definitions is aggressively reasserted. Across the range of available imagery we are provided with a basic picture, a shape, which indicates the coherent, closed-off unit we instantly 'know' to be a family.

Here are groups of people of assorted ages and sexes, touching, clutching, all smiles to the camera. Heads tilted towards each other, wanting to be photographed, wanting to be recorded in *this* position, in precisely *this* relation to each of the others, offering themselves together for the viewer to acknowledge. Each person in this basic image is carefully placed, arranged according to age and sex: adults above, children below. Older children, preferably boys, best aligned with the man; younger children, girls and babies, tend to line up with the woman. The sexes are clearly differentiated by clothing,

Leaflet FIS.1   November 1977

Family income supplement

Nationwide
Building Society

Annual Report & Accounts
1980

Country classics

One look at the superb quality of the YOU
Magazine classic country jacket and you'll
understand why...

YOU MAGAZINE OFFER

Now-you can knit everything for your family

easier, quicker and at a fraction of shop prices!

Authentic Arran—and the world's best traditional patterns—easy with CREATIVE KNITTERS

Paris Exclusive! Make it yourself tailor-made for you.

Practical 'Bomber' jacket he'll love to wear.

Luxurious car rug or over blanket.

Delightful cuddly toys - for a few pence

NEW

Creative Knitters Club

with the Guaranteed
Tried-and-tested Patterns Service

SEE INSIDE FOR GREAT STARTER KIT WORTH £2.00

length of hair and props – girls' toys or boys' toys. They present themselves as an indissoluble unit, as if gummed together, to make one shape outlined in the total presentation, surrounded by nothingness or an out-of-focus background.

It is a configuration that has withstood time. Despite changes in family ideology and actual patterns of living over the last twenty years, building societies, publicity brochures and magazine covers have continued to recycle this basic image and variations on it. Recently the group has become slightly more fluid in its arrangement, but the biggest change has been that since the end of the 1980s, it often falls to the man to hold the baby.

The power of these pictures lies in their ability to call up an abstract concept. They are a visible representation of that group of a man and a woman of one generation, legally tied to each other in an exclusive sexual relationship, living in a single household with the children of both of them. The pictures may show 'real' named individuals, or models employed to play the part. Either way, we sense an element of staging – of conscious re-enactment – in the construction of the image. Each individual performs the part expected of them, and it is essential to the singularity of the unit that each plays a *different* part. The pictures are like diagrams of relationships, maps which accept the flat plane of the printed page. They indicate four possible positions, and place within each a representation of a physical body.

In the most basic form of the image, the male half is consistently larger than the female half. Children are rarely allowed to age above twelve and remain well below their parents in height and well within their physical control. Examples which spoil the map or add ambiguity are excluded, so that the differences themselves produce the expected relations of power and subordination. The hands of the adults touch and restrain the children, who nevertheless offer no resistance to their positioning. We may not be able to name the members of the group, but we can instantly *label* them – Father, Mother, Son, Daughter. In making this recognition we do more than give our consent to a set of social arrangements; we take an active part in renewing a particular, limited meaning of 'family'. The image becomes not just a picture of an ideal family or a perfect family, but the very meaning of 'family' itself.

The family group is separated off from the outside world, and the encircling arms of the man at its apex mark its boundaries. The direction of the touch is from him, towards them. He is the only one who remains unenclosed, the woman's arm often lost beneath his dominating shoulder. His body marks the transition between an exterior, public world and an interior, private one. He has the power to define a space and to limit the ways in which others may be present in it. From his position at the apex of the group, he draws from its members expressions of pleasure and affirmation. Their smiling faces demonstrate their assent to their positioning without hint of discord. His touch confirms the physicality of their pleasure but prevents the uncontrollable chaos of the erotic from emerging. He holds the group in place. As well as being pictures of a family, these are pictures of a man.

A line drawing may reduce the image to its bare essentials, standing on the page like a hieroglyph, the pictorial equivalent of a word, unhindered by fleshy existence. Even the most perfectly staged of photographs may be disrupted by the excessive, the unexpected and the unwanted, but a drawing can control these dangers. By condensing its meanings into a simplified pictorial shape, it can create the impression that they are fixed and inevitable, difficult to resist. Consequently, when we speak of a 'family' a visual lumber of meanings comes trailing behind, bringing a cluster of ideas whch determine what we say before we begin to say it. *This* kind of family arranged in *this* way dominates attempts to think of alternatives.

Pictures of children within the family group are made by almost everyone. Cameras which are cheap, easy to use and small enough to be a regular part of holiday baggage, together with high-speed film which gives reliable results in rich and gratifying colour, have made possible an ever more varied range of domestic pictures. The snapshot creates its own prolific imagery of childhood. Our family albums revive warm memories and a nostalgia for a past that is part reality, part fantasy. Leafing through its pages, we recall pleasures we have lived, people we have loved and, most poignantly of all, our earlier selves. But these are pictures which gain their power only as we stitch them into the fabric of our personal history. They depend for their meaning on our identification and recognition of their subjects. Therefore, when an advertisement uses the snapshot style, not only does it reach for a warmth that belongs to more familiar faces, it encourages us to see *our* loved ones in its anonymous public figures, and to work on its pictures as we do on our own. We enhance the public image with emotions from our private pictures and, in a reciprocal move, our memories are themselves enhanced, as advertisements, particularly those for photographic products, offer a repertoire of family characters and family moments. Even the technology of domestic photography – the medium lens, the fixed focus – disposes its users to produce pictures that will suit the intimate family group.

Over its hundred-year history, Kodak has encouraged millions of home photographers to domesticate their imaginations and use their frozen memories to reaffirm a family setting. While family pictures notoriously recall different emotions for the different individuals held within the frame, in the public image any restlessness, unhappiness or possibility of multiple perspectives is smoothed over. The work of the image is to combat the danger of disintegration, and that work centres on the children. How can we deny the appeal of such confident smiles? They defy us to spoil their enjoyment, and challenge us to share their happiness, to echo their confidence and security within our own less perfect group.

When the family poses together, each person directs their separate smile at the camera and the viewers. They use special, self-approving smiles, as if each were admiring their own reflection in a mirror, creating a picture for their own posterity in a notional album. The smiles confirm the group as the centre of a pleasure which is contingent not on individual character or behaviour, but on the satisfactory composition of the family itself. However, there are pictures of families in which the smiles may be questioned, where the presentation is less confident and the symmetry is lost. Such

families are accompanied by texts which note the breaking of the pattern. They may be too big or too diverse. The children may be multiple births, mixed-race or adopted. Too many children lead to a reduction of the parents' ability to dominate. In a Health Education Council leaflet, the adults disappear among the crowd. Although the number of working mothers, the number of divorces and the use of childminders and nannies are all increasing, the absence of either parent, particularly the mother, is shown as a problem which leads to troublesome children. A disturbance in the traditional roles of mother and father has led to recurring moral panics.

Paradoxically, the only person who can be satisfactorily absent from the structured family is the father himself. He can be outside the picture without losing control when it is he who, as seems so natural, 'takes' the snap. For him it becomes an image of his possessions, his people. Inside the frame he can enclose with his arms, but from the outside he can create the frame itself, enclosing with his directing eye. But there is another important reason for his reduction in importance. His absence means the all-important presence of consumer goods. Routine departures for a daily job can be compensated for with routine goods, but an extreme absence in Tokyo or Bombay needs something more dramatic – like a diamond. Of course, as the insurance advertisements remind him, his total absence is irreplaceable. His is a position that cannot be delegated. Left alone, his wife can only 'struggle on'. He can be satisfactorily replaced only by money. In this symbolic system, the power of the father and the power of money become interchangeable.

So the imagery shows the perfect family group to be not so perfect after all. It creates a lack by its very existence. 'Families need . . .' is a recurring phrase in the language of advertising. To keep the smile in place, families need goods. Without them, they are nothing. Compare the perfection of a Barclays insurance leaflet from the late 1970s – the intricate detail of the clothes, the comfortable home, the expensive car, the food and leisure equipment – with the contemporary leaflet issued by the DHSS to publicise Family Income Supplement. The family on a low income is virtually simplified out of existence. Its members are nothing but empty shapes. Not only are there no smiles, there are no faces. The perfect circle is flawed, the pleasure of consumption tempered by the effort needed to make that consumption possible – not to lose face. The 1979 leaflet is perhaps its most extreme visual expression, but the stark contrast between consumer plenitude and welfare austerity has, if anything, increased as poorer families have become even more difficult to imagine, and risk disappearing from the imagery altogether.

To peep in on a family group and catch its members as they are absorbed in their daily lives, many advertisements draw on a different tradition of photography. Making a snapshot is a collective activity, but taking a documentary picture means photographing others without their knowledge. A snapshot is intended to remind us of events and people we know; a documentary picture offers us information about those who are unknown. The snapshot depends on our memory; the documentary claims to be complete in itself. It captures the unguarded moment, peers into forbidden places and does not hesitate to uncover truths the participants may prefer to conceal. The codes of photographic naturalism – people have their backs to the camera, are frozen in the middle of activity and appear awkward or ungainly – give these advertisements their sense of authenticity.

Documentary pictures claim to show life as it is – and we have reason to be apprehensive as they invite us into the secret places of the family. For we are well aware of the ugly underside, the dark and dangerous emotions which lurk within family relationships. Yet these presentations reveal . . . perfection. We see happiness, laughter and relaxation, always secured by the joyful presence of children at play. We see affluence and abundance in well-furnished homes, gilded by that ubiquitous family smile. This is the moment of perfect satisfaction we feared we could never attain. We welcome such pictures with grateful hearts. These precious moments are captured in the home or some family playground – a beach, a country lane or a village green. The car is a recurring feature, acting as a mobile home to transport the family between its two locations.

With Pakistan International Airlines, it's just like coming home. There's nothing better.

GREEN SHIELD stamps

for you, your family and your home...

You know the feeling. It's a warm smile. A relaxed atmosphere. A lot of caring. You can be yourself. Just like home.

The feeling begins when you step aboard our big friendly aircraft. Our big birds. B747s, DC10s and now, the much applauded wide-bodied A300, powered by whisper-quiet General Electric engines.

A home-coming to over 60 destinations, on four continents, around the world.

When next you fly to America, Europe, the Middle East, Africa or Asia, fly Pakistan International Airlines.

You will feel like you're coming home.

PIA
Great people to fly with

The home itself is the dream house of all aspiring homeowners. It usually has a rural aspect, with a big garden, mullioned windows and a Virginia creeper. Its interior is lit by a warm glow – a glint of sunlight or firelight. Colours are rich browns, reds and yellows, emphasising the highly polished table tops and well-brushed carpets. Presentations like those found in sales catalogues and consumer magazines are crammed with as many domestic objects as possible. Possessions take up the centre of the picture, with the family spread around them. Physical contact is extended through the goods that link its members with each other. They stretch their arms over and across them, reaching towards one another but touching the car, sofa, parcel or catalogue. The gestures of reaching and handling may replace the exchange of looks. Although looks are directed between members, they often seem to miss, fly past, or fail to engage or elicit a response. Nevertheless, the wholeness of the group is confirmed by the presence of all the members – and often a dog, too – and by the familiar, familial smile. No one withholds their commitment or the intensity of their enjoyment. 'You know the feeling,' the advertisement for Pakistan International Airlines reminds us. 'It's a warm smile. A relaxed atmosphere. A lot of caring. You can be yourself.'

Being yourself in the charmed circle of home means different things for the differentiated members of the group. Men express relaxation; women are more likely to be busy at their tasks. It is clear that these perfect homes and well-dressed children, with their shining hair and remarkable cleanliness, are maintained by the love of a woman. When a child changes a couple into a family and a woman into a mother, her sexuality is visibly modified and her love of necessity changes its form. The constant presence of young children in the family image controls the sexual behaviour of the parents, and the absence of teenagers prevents the question from being reintroduced. Thus, while keeping the mess and disruption of sex at bay, the woman is seen to transform her love into care for the children and the home. Cleanliness and cleansing rituals play a central role in protecting the purity of childhood within the family context. In pictures of the family at play, everyone glows with health. Disability or illness is visible only if a special point is being made. Of course, rumbustious children are accident-prone and any child is prey to whatever bug is going round the classroom, but this, too, can soon be put right by the mother – aided by a spoonful of the appropriate concoction.

But a child creates a family, and it falls to the pictured children to secure the domestic idyll and bring about the warmth and mutual pleasures the imagery seeks to create. Safe within the orderly structure of the group, the children provide its emotive outlet. It is they who may leap and run; their facial expressions show least restraint. Their visible instability and vulnerability are the ultimate justification for the family itself – but at the same time they hold the potential to shatter the harmonious image as it touches the edge of what is tolerable.

Within the proper limits of the family, the carefree pleasures of childhood are celebrated as a value in themselves, their tendency to excess is made safe. But these mobile bodies are also performing a political and economic role – taking on themselves the stresses of a changing social regime. Children, we are told in cheerfully illustrated features on fashion and advertising trends, are at the cutting edge of market expansion. In consequence, in catalogues and fashion pages, advertisements and sales brochures, children have leapt free from their backgrounds, beyond familial constraints, their activity legitimised by context of commerce alone. A boom in children's goods – and especially children's fashions – has meant that experienced child models are in demand. 'The children must live within easy reach of London, have photogenic qualities, be outgoing but not precocious and not disablingly shy', wrote Annalena McAfee, herself a former child model. As they romp through the fashion features of the 1990s,

loosely arranged against neutral backgrounds, the stress is on the child rather than the context. No fake documentary realism here, just the intensity of movement condensed into small, energetic bodies. As expenditure on children has increased, so has the frenzy of the image. 'Kiddie fashion' now ranges from tutu and black velvet to what one writer described as 'rap, nouveau hippie and environmental influences' – preferably all mixed together, combining knowing sophistication with childish fun. The kaleidoscopic colour and clutter of shapes and fancies which previously added excitement to pictures of parties now decorate the bodies of children themselves.

This image of bodily freedom comes at a time when children's independent movement is limited by an ever-present sense of public danger. The streetwise image became current as children were kept firmly off the streets and transported by car whenever possible. There is a striking contrast between the Levis advertisements of 1979, set in adventure playgrounds and against graffitied walls, and the presentations of the 1990s. Children's clothes of the 1970s claimed to be practical and hard-wearing; the tough kids called out 'Come and be in our gang'. The Bermuda shorts, designer T-shirts and baseball caps of the 1990s are bought for their fashion points. Far from forming gangs, the children who wear them pose separately, with little relation to each other. The Advertising Standards Authority's code of practice relating to children specifically forbids them to be shown engaging in any dangerous activity or in any situation that exposes them to danger – like playing in the street, 'unless it is clearly shown to be a play street or other safe area'. A context of price tags, shopping information and design devices poses no such problem. Backgrounds may indicate street culture with a few stagey props. In their multicoloured clothing and their multicultural groups, these model children present an image which confuses freedom with bodily movement and satisfaction with the pleasure of possession.

'Children's pocket money is much in demand', *Campaign* told readers who were interested in the bubble gum and cheap confectionery market. Pocket money for children whose parents have comfortable incomes is rising all the time, but larger items must be designed to appeal both to the children and to those who buy for them. In other words, they must convey something of the way children see themselves, and something of the way parents see them. There remains a striking difference between the fangs, blood, skulls and lavatorial humour of items designed for children to buy with their own money, and the educational toys and tasteful tracksuits targeted at their parents. For manufacturers are now marketing to parents who have borne their children in their executive thirties instead of their impoverished twenties. In 1989 the Royal Society for the Prevention of Accidents estimated that each of Britain's ten million children under fourteen receives on average twenty new toys each year. The *Mail on Sunday* displayed under-fives surrounded by their possessions – toys totalling between £1,000 and £2,000 in value when new. Since children are outside the exacting sequence of earning, saving and expenditure, it seems as if there are no constraints on their enjoyment of their new clothes and toys, and their chocolate bars, cornflakes, baked beans, ice creams, Sugar Pops, Hula Hoops, fizzy drinks and the rest of the tooth-rotting products on offer. Their mouths are always open for the next enticing snack.

Have your kids earned their bar today?

Children's inability to defer gratification threatens their parents' purse and often their parents' sense of the proper limits to consumption. But well-provided pre-teens – already owners of personal stereos, computers and bicycles as well as their well-stocked and constantly renewed wardrobes – are in training to be a new kind of adult. As children negotiate their tastes with the parents who buy for them, it is the parents who are learning to defer to children's wishes, recognising in them an accession to adulthood in a market-orientated world. The image is working to harness children's joys and sorrows to their new role as discriminating consumers. Is this an exploitation of childhood, as some commentators argue, or is it the triumph of those libidinous values that, until now, children have been required to express on behalf of us all? In these presentations their desires are always satisfied. Adults are partly bullied, partly seduced, as the pictured child produces a repertoire of persuasive behaviour. The threat is always just beneath the surface. That hyperactivity could so easily become a behavioural problem, and that lovable pout transform itself into an uncontrollable temper tantrum.

Advertising imagery has no space for families which fail, and little space for those which don't conform. But pictures of families of the famous – a staple of the tabloid press and the feature pages of the consumer magazines – can show the whole range of single parents, extended families, late children, adopted children, in a celebration of the variety of family life. The instant popularity of the photo-gossip magazine *Hello!*, launched in 1988, must surely be due to a fascination with such unpredictable family stories – particularly when they are about the rich and when they always turn out for the best. 'We're not going to run unpleasant pictures or say unpleasant things about anyone', said editor Maggie Goodman. Its lushly coloured pages regularly feature bouncing, well-fed and beautiful children. The support that money can buy, which makes such variety possible, is visible in the opulence of the settings, but never in the people who maintain them. Once more the one person who never figures in these pictures is perhaps the most indispensable of all: the nanny.

The most popular of all public pictures are still those of the Royal family and their Royal children. Always moving with the times, the Royal soap opera continues to hold the nation enthralled. These most privileged of children and their mothers, fathers, grandmothers, aunts and uncles are both very special and reassuringly ordinary. They share our flaws – and we can't take our eyes off them.

The sense of continuity and stability created by families whose cohesion over the generations is ensured by their wealth and status itself puts pressure on our concept of family, trailing behind it a petty snobbery that can itself be commodified. For a few pounds anyone can have the genealogy of their surname traced back, and be provided with a coat of arms or a parchment scroll as proof of antiquity. The aristocratic family, with its family trees, its ancestral portraits and its ownership of stately homes and tracts of land, appears in popular discourse as a culturally valued protector of history and tradition. From this perspective the child becomes the focus for the future, not of the human race, but of a limited and competitive unit. At a time when large numbers of ordinary people can expect to inherit wealth – if only in the form of a 1930s semi or a mortgaged ex-council house – the idea of inheritance has taken on a new life. The central figure is that of the father, for it is he who passes on his name and money. He can protect the future of 'his' family through investment and insurance. It seems natural that advertisements for such services should use pictures of children. Childhood takes on a more practical relationship with the future when the child stands to inherit money or material goods.

The theme of biological inheritance overlaps with that of material inheritance – in both, the 'natural' father is all-important. Divorce, adoption and reproductive technologies are separating the biological acts of conception and giving birth from the social continuity of childcare, and making links with the 'natural' father more tenuous and remote. The 1975 Children's Act gave adopted children the right to seek their 'real' identity, and the late 1980s saw a spate of articles on that search for biological 'reality'. The discovery that a 'real' father was an anonymous sperm donor was considered to be deeply traumatic. Artificial Insemination by Donor (AID) was described in the *Sunday Times* as 'sowing the seeds of despair'. But AID treatment for a woman who had never had sexual intercourse was the ultimate outrage. 'Ban virgin births', demanded the London *Evening Standard* in April 1991.

In the ideal image a child must have two 'natural' parents, and the father remains the pivotal point. It is a position that is in no way challenged by contemporary attempts to soften the image of fatherhood, or to add a child as a lifestyle accessory to expand the scope of masculinity. A 1991 Volvo advertisement shows a classic four-

position family spread around their car – except that both adult positions are occupied by the same man. He appears, as we have come to expect, with the signs of his leisure – his tennis racquets and his sports bag. But he is also placed beside his children. We are enabled to see them as entertaining leisure companions rather than demanding creatures who need feeding, dressing and nursing when they're sick. The person who will tend to those needs is banished from this narcissistic image. 'Satisfy your other half' reads the slogan, whose ambiguity neatly defuses criticism.

The 'family' remains a protected image, defining its own protected space. The surrounding structures which enable that image – or some approximation to it – to flourish in the real world – such things as the availability of benefits, the possibility of unemployment, the quality of health care and housing – are pushed to the margins of the dominant imagery. But these are the conditions that determine the ability of 'parents' – whether adoptive parents, single parents, married couples, working mothers or childminders – to secure the well-being of the children in their care. They surface elsewhere in the available imagery, in a much more muted form, described as social problems or political issues.

The disturbances which threaten from within – the fear of violence, of inappropriate sexuality of children who are uncontrollable, sullen or destructive, or who simply don't fit the picture of what children 'should' be like – all these possibilities leave traces which, paradoxically, contribute to the pleasure of presentations designed, above all, to please. Once more, they are elaborated on elsewhere in the imagery. For the moment, we are likely to take these laughing children and their happy families at their own valuation.

SATISFY YOUR OTHER HALF.

Now here's a Volvo well able to cater for your more adventurous self.

Couched under the bonnet is an intercooled, turbo charged engine that develops 119 bhp.

An electronic boost control ensures a smooth and rapid power response. For the technically minded this means negligible turbo lag and a virtually flat torque curve.

As a consequence the 50-70 mph top gear acceleration of 11.2 seconds surpasses that of the Peugeot 405 Mi16, the BMW 520i 24-Valve and the Mazda MX5.

So your other half will have the performance just when it's needed.

To cater for your more protective instincts, a servo assisted ABS braking system is fitted as standard.

As also, are the rigid steel safety cage, front and rear crumple zones and side impact safety bars.

Add to that power steering, electric windows, light alloy wheels, rear spoiler and an electronic information centre and what do you have?

A Volvo with the power to satisfy the most demanding other half. **THE VOLVO 440 TURBO.**

3

Ignorant pupils and harmonious nature

Learning to play or playing to learn?

Over the last twenty years, images of schoolchildren have been at the centre of many an acrimonious debate. Different definitions of childhood require different types of schooling. 'Children are not born good,' declared Conservative MP and ex-headmaster Sir Rhodes Boyson. 'They have to be disciplined, otherwise they're a threat to the rest of society.' As one of the contributors to the first *Black Paper on Education* in 1968, Rhodes Boyson was one of the initiators of a twenty-year campaign which changed the direction of educational policy and culminated in the Education Reform Act of 1988. While most schools have continued to exercise a pragmatic accommodation between different theories of education and balanced educational requirements against available resources, the popular press has produced images of childhood and schooling within sharply polarised positions, as if lined up for battle.

In contemporary discourse, both 'school' and 'education' are rich in implications. The two concepts sometimes overlap, sometimes conflict with each other. Some say schools inhibit education rather than facilitating it; for others the two are interchangeable, as if the physical location itself ensures the activity. The importance of school depends on which educational aims are valued most highly, and debates around the purpose of education dash against its contradictory aspirations. Is it a mechanism for social training or a channel for personal fulfilment? It promises both. It can enable latent talents to bloom, and it can elevate in social status. It can open the door to

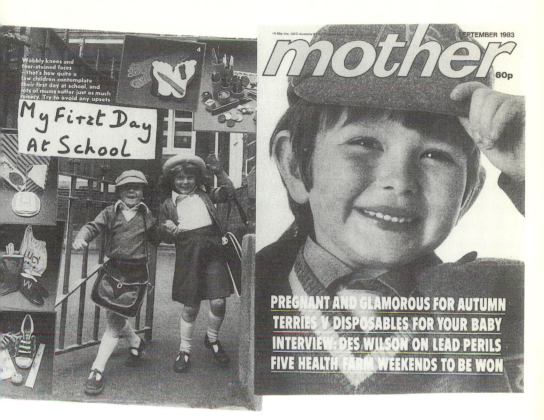

SEPTEMBER 1983

mother

60p

Wobbly knees and
tear-stained faces
—that's how quite a
few children contemplate
their first day at school, and
lots of mums suffer just as much
misery. Try to avoid any upsets

**My First Day
At School**

**PREGNANT AND GLAMOROUS FOR AUTUMN
TERRIES V DISPOSABLES FOR YOUR BABY
INTERVIEW: DES WILSON ON LEAD PERILS
FIVE HEALTH FARM WEEKENDS TO BE WON**

cultural riches, but must, in the words of the Department of Education and Science, 'satisfy the needs of an advanced technological
country, competing in international markets'. It must prepare for
unemployment as well as employment, and teach how to spend as
well as how to earn. When a child first leaves the private world of the
home and enters the public space of the school, the tensions around
the final outcome of his or her education are already visible.

The first image of school is one that mediates that unavoidable
transition. It reassures worried parents that all will be well, and that
their aspirations will be satisfied. The authors of *Unpopular Education*
have argued that since the introduction of compulsory schooling in
the late nineteenth century, educational policy has been concerned
essentially with the education of the working class. In the second half
of the twentieth century it has been the perspective of the upwardly
mobile segment of the working class that has dominated popular
opinion on education and schooling. The view that achievement and
social improvement are attainable only through schooling has underpinned popular narratives of the last twenty years. Schools are seen

as offering children a precious value which parents have reached out for but failed to grasp. Children go to school not to follow their own desires, but to live out the desires of someone else – indeed, of almost everyone else. The tentative looks on the faces of the five-year-olds in their new school clothes are expressing a major social concern. It is up to them to grasp the importance of school for society but, at the same time, to reconstruct it as the pathway to their personal future.

The theme of happiness dominates the discourse of the primary school, a happiness that will sustain the links between children and their parents even as they depart through the school gates. 'If he (or she) is happy, then you're laughing', a presentation from *Parents* magazine told its readers. As children grow older, such reflection of the parents' desire in their faces becomes less possible, and the imagery of childhood moves into a new phase.

The institutions of family and school put forward competing definitions of childhood. Both construct a childhood with no independent validity and little independent existence. It is the nature of this dependence and incompleteness which is at issue, and the conflict is expressed in the imagery. When a child appears as a pupil, a gradual calming of the image begins – a latency period between the euphoria of early childhood and the chaos of youth. The child's body is encased in special clothing and encumbered with equipment which signifies the need for discipline and the need to learn. The image emphasises those qualities children lack – the knowledge, understanding and competencies of adult life. It is the job of the professionals of education to make good these childish lacks but, paradoxically, they must also protect them, for children must not be deprived of their childhood too soon. In the double function of dividing childhood from adulthood and of forming a bridge between the two, as much effort goes into enforcing the separation as into enabling the transition.

Separation from the adult world means that the characteristics of schoolchildren threaten to contaminate the adults who surround them. They may be sucked into the whirlpool of uncontrolled childishness unless they have been properly trained and taught to withstand the dangers and impose classroom discipline. Popular narratives remind us that teachers' methods may be too esoteric for outsiders to understand. While children at school may be gregarious among themselves, they are forbidden unstructured contact with adults. Opportunities for informal learning or for accidental adjustments to adult values must be reduced. Professional teaching and orderly learning characterise the classroom.

Mothers are shown to be deeply puzzled and concerned. 'Their' children are no longer under their control but that of trained specialists. Their rights over their children are dramatically curtailed.

Family relationships must be readjusted in accordance with social institutions and legal requirements.

In presentations from the 1970s to the 1990s – especially in September, when the new generation leaves for school for the first time – five-to-seven-year-olds make their farewell gestures from advertisements for school uniforms and the pages of parents' magazines. The axis of the family image is swung round, so that the exchange of smiles is no longer within the frame but between pictured child and viewing parent. These generalised children, child models, stand in for all youngsters as they leave their homes, smiling reassuringly at 'their' mothers. Real-life mothers, responding to these engaging, perfect pictures, may thereby ease their worries about their own, much more problematic, flesh-and-blood girls and boys.

Their faces reassure, but the symbolic presentation of the children is in the process of readjustment. The regime of the school has already taken over their bodies. Their playful gestures contrast with the dark skirts and school hats and the heavy loads they must now carry with them. Parents are expected to provide the equipment and clothing which themselves symbolise the contest of rights and definitions – satchels, pencils, notebooks, sensible shoes, clean shirts and smart blazers. The well-equipped schoolchild appears as a shiny surface, washed, polished and brushed, a credit to those who service him/her. To produce a child in this image is the job of the servicing mother, and in doing so she services the school itself. The smiles in the picture are necessary to maintain her relationship with her children and her support for the school regime. As the child disappears through the gates, the individual becomes one of a group and the indulgent parent's eye contemplating the image of the child is replaced by the eye of the critical teacher.

To realise its promise, the school must enclose this child – and all children – within its boundaries, and children must be subject to its control. The space of school must be kept separate from that of the family and clearly differentiated from it. Unlike a 'family', made up of members of different ages and sexes, schools contain large numbers of the same type of person gathered together in a limited and clearly defined space. Pictures which seek to represent 'school' search for images of multiplicity. Their frames are filled with many children, gregariously bunched together, engaged in similar activities, leading to similar ends. Racial and ethnic differences are unimportant in this collecting together by age. These children are unnamed exemplars. Each one represents its generation. On entering school, a child becomes one of a type.

The gathering together of children carries dangers of its own. There is the danger inherent in crowding itself, in promiscuous contact with numerous others. Assembled together, children may develop autonomous activities which exclude adults. They may egg each other on or form into gangs. Their uproar and mobility are aggravated by their numbers, so that it is important to keep track of a single individual for every moment of time. School becomes a place where order and disorder confront each other. In the imagery of school there is always a visual effort to present children as a *purposeful* group, to convert the incipient disorder of the crowd into what Michel Foucault described as a 'disciplinary society'. For Foucault, 'The principle of "enclosure" is neither constant, nor indispensable, nor sufficient in disciplinary machinery. This machinery works space in a much more flexible and detailed way.' He outlines some of the principles of 'disciplinary space': 'Each individual has his own place and each place its individual. Avoid distributions in groups; break up collective dispositions; analyse confused, massive or transient pluralities. Disciplinary space tends to be divided into as many sections as there are bodies or elements to be distributed. Any teacher would endorse the effort to 'eliminate the effects of imprecise distributions, the uncontrolled disap-pearance of individuals, their diffuse circulation, their unstable and dangerous coagulation'.

To achieve this orderly regime, childish spontaneity, which is so highly valued in the family imagery, must take on negative conno-tations. The restlessness of childhood, its random and purposeless movement, indicates precisely those qualities that school is designed to change. It now becomes naughtiness, inattention or downright disobedience. Above all, on entering school children give up their right to undirected play. Activities which seem like play must be redefined as images of learning. Much of the imagery of the child in the primary schools deals with the complexities of this redefinition. It must balance the concepts of 'play', 'learning' and 'work' – so similar and yet so different from each other. 'Learning' is the only work permitted to children, since adult, productive work is forbid-den to them, but learning is more acceptable if it looks like work rather than play.

The subversive possibility of play invading the disciplinary space of the school has given rise to acute public anxiety, but parents are increasingly encouraged to make the reverse movement and import learning back into the home. 'To him it's just a toy. To you it's the beginning of his education', toy manufacturers Fisher Price told parents shopping for their toddlers. For the children there is an element of deception involved – the ulterior motive is invisible to them. For parents the learning child has become the acceptable face of the consuming child. The dangers of play for its own sake are tamed, and children's participation in the economic process is

"Mummy, I can read!"

Give your child a head-start in the most important subject of them all – before he starts school.

The joy of learning...

24 Number activities

Each month, two activities help your child to group objects, and understand the idea of counting, stage by stage, with the use of rhymes and pictures.

48 Speech activities

Each month, four activities encourage and stimulate your child's speech development, with the aid of rhymes, speech-sounds, tongue-twisters and stories.

48 Pre-reading activities

Each month, four activities help your child to understand the relationship between shapes, sizes, colours and words; to identify common objects and fit them into story situations. Each activity helps prepare your child for reading . . .

FREE, with Month One: A colourfully illustrated Elmfo[...] Village street-pl[...] in scale with the press-out mo[...] buildings. (I[...] with most [...] cars, [...] Size: [...] x [...]

tempered by a more sober image. All the world may be a classroom, but what is shown is the home filled with the lumber of consumer goods. High Street toy shops have obligingly transformed themselves into Early Learning Centres and homes which purchase educational toys, musical instruments and learning-to-read kits remain distinguishable from those whose consumption is passive and morally suspect – who buy videos, sound systems and large-screen TVs. Books remain an important sign which link education, culture and fine living – nicely parodied in the imitation tooled-leather boxes made for that more dubious medium, the videotape.

The potency of the book, the printed word, and its superiority as an instrument of learning, allows the institution for which books are a central symbol to criticise and intervene in inappropriate homes characterised as bookless. Over the years government reports on education and the writings of pundits have criticised homes where consumption is orientated to pleasure and relaxation rather than to self-improvement and learning. In such homes, children may be at risk of moving directly from the dangerous realm of disorganised play to the equally dangerous realm of productive work. Education can rescue them from these hazards.

'Parents in the manual occupational group show signs of alienation from the schools their children attend', wrote J.M. Bynner in a government report on parents' attitudes to education in 1972. 'They provide the weakest educational support for their children . . . their homes show least evidence of literacy . . . Some of these parents' other attitudes are out of step with those of the school. Of all parents, they are the most likely to be in favour of their children having part-time jobs . . . ' No wonder the mothers looking at the image of the departing child are worried!

However, consumer hedonism began to take precedence over middle-class moralism, and the language of class became outmoded. The overlap between play, learning and work was pulled sharply apart in a different way. The working-class home is now encouraged to assert its consumer rights in the 'parental choice' of schools. The argument, put by educational reformers in the free-market wing of the Conservative Party, assumes that such parents will clearly opt for schools where the issue is not fudged. It was seen as the final vindication of the view expressed in the very first *Black Paper*: that unlike the middle classes, who remain bemused by educational theory, 'working-class parents know how to distinguish between play and work'.

The Plowden Report, written at approximately the same time, had taken a diametrically opposite view, and confirmed what was to become the orthodoxy for primary classrooms: 'This distinction between work and play is false, possibly throughout life, certainly in the primary school . . . Play is the central activity in all nursery schools and many infant schools.' Throughout the 1970s and 1980s the popular press mounted increasingly scathing attacks on this 'progressive' approach, describing it as evidence of subversive left-wing intervention in the education system. The shifting territory covered by 'work', 'play' and 'learning' became a battleground.

The dominant imagery of the 1970s showed child-centred education of the Plowden type. It is best exemplified by pictures in magazines like the Inner London Education Authority's *Contact*, distributed free to the Authority's teacher employees. In the 1970s it was a substantial magazine, printed on glossy paper, with many pages in full colour. Concerned educationists were presented with visual and verbal image of their work and the children in their care. *Contact* made use of the action-documentary style of photograph, with children 'captured' in the midst of their activities, their variety emphasised by the use of many small frames arranged on a unifying page in the manner of a family album. The pictures show a cheerful bustle and clutter. Each frame is filled with the active bodies of children and a rich profusion of objects spread around them for their use. Rabbits, building bricks, paints, Plasticine, new technology – the eclecticism is matched by richness of the colour. But this activity is far from indiscriminate and uncontrolled. Every object has not only its place but also its label. Their pedagogic purpose structures the movements of the children. Every detail has a part to play in the enterprise of learning.

The magazine itself recognised that the activity of learning was not immediately visible, and instructed its readers on how to interpret both the image and the primary classroom itself. They should not be misled by the apparently unstructured bustle of the group, but should note 'the degree of involvement of the individual child and the work habits acquired', and especially 'the efforts of the teacher to inculcate good habits of orderliness and the necessary persistence to complete a task successfully and learn the correct attitudes of tidiness'. Constantly working near the borders of discipline, this primary-school classroom must be read as a major achievement of

SPOTLIGHT

ELEANOR PALMER PRIMARY SCHOOL,

Lupton Street, Tufnell Park, NW5.

The Headmaster, Mr M. G. Holding, writes:
This is a one form entry multi-racial school of 250 children and 10 teachers comprising infant and juniors sections.

The younger classes are vertically grouped and the children remain with their first teacher for up to two years. The infant section pursues an integrated day. The third year attends Kentish Town Library and the learner swimming pool at the Prince of Wales Baths.

Believing that success in the basic subjects is a necessary basis for all education, the children in the junior school are taught English and Mathematics for one hour each day in sets according to their ability. This provides considerable flexibility in grouping, and gives the children beneficial changes of teachers.

Our older children compete in all local sports competitions and all children have

discipline. It is designed to challenge and defuse the dangers of disorder and lack of control. It faces the challenge of play head on and converts it into work through learning. Plowden's view was that learning should be 'in harmony with the nature of the child' and that the child's nature would bring its own order. These pictures are an image of that harmony.

Teachers and pupils are presented as collaborators in the enterprise of the school. Conflict between them seems unthinkable. Indeed, for Plowden the best teacher was an invisible one, internalised in the children. She could leave the room and the class would carry on without noticing. Not surprisingly, teachers rarely dominate these pictures. They are either absent or their heads rise only slightly above the bent heads of the children. When pictures of a progressive classroom centre on the teacher, we find them either holding the rapt attention of a group of delighted youngsters, or *behind* the group, encouraging them, initiating and sharing their activity.

Visible or not, the teacher remains the controlling centre. The right to look is theirs alone. From outside the frame, theirs are the eyes that shape the classroom and its contents. The practice of observation and documentation of children's activities is at the centre of progressive pedagogy. The exchange of looks between teacher and pupil is by no means reciprocal. While teachers watch children to control and guide them, children may look at teachers only in ways that indicate their status as pupils. They must respond when the teacher addresses them directly and attend when the whole class is being taught. At all times they must be totally available for professional observation, and reveal themselves without artifice. They should forgo the temptation to adopt a 'mask of seemliness' (Maria Montessori's phrase) or indeed any other mask, and present themselves without strategies for self-protection.

This one-way relationship has much in common with the relationship that structures documentary photography. The photographer, too, aims to look where the look is not returned and where the subjects of the picture are unaware of the photographic gaze, producing photographs which deny the presence of the observer and seek to produce a report that will be objective and non-partisan. The careful selection of pictures presents a vision of harmony. The dangerous ambiguities of play are smoothed out; school refusal, bullying and boredom become invisible. Resistance to the teacher's controlling gaze – refusal to occupy the allotted space, refusal to look the teacher in the eye – simply do not appear. The possibility of learning outside the controlled environment and the possibility of secret places away from the teacher's observation are ignored. A pragmatic social-democratic politics, in which the guidance of educated professionals plays an important part, has been associated with both the documentary movement – with its aim to provide clear, unbiased information – and the progressive classroom – with its commitment to improving facilities for the underprivileged and playing down differences in ability and attainment. But this dual stress on the responsibility of the professionals and egalitarian politics brought progressivism increasingly under attack by campaigners on behalf of traditional teaching and formal assessment. The question was asked: Who has the right to observe the teachers?

The child-centred classroom became an object of scorn for an unsympathetic press, for whom a confusion between work and play was symptomatic of both disorder and political subversion: 'Gone are the two-by-two rows of desks. Pupils sit haphazardly grouped at work tables – a doubtful improvement when it comes to a handwriting class in one South London Junior school, where, because of the table arrangement, one half of the class were sitting with their backs to the blackboard.' So wrote Joanna Patyna in the London *Evening News*. The campaign was on to change the image, to get the teacher back at the front of the class and the desks in orderly lines facing the blackboard. The preferred image of a 'traditional' classroom associated itself with educational standards which must be imposed on children rather than drawn out of them. In this view their potential for wildness is such that they cannot be trusted to internalise disciplinary norms. The nature of the child is far from harmonious, and the politics are those of competition and the free market.

For the traditionalists, children need training, clear-cut structures and punishment where necessary. The changing imagery of school illustrates this conflict between internal and external constraint. In the one the body of the child is controlled by the disciplines of the mind; in the other by the disciplines of the regime. Each image deals in its own way with the twin moments of liberation and control.

By the mid 1980s, the traditional view of schooling was strongly reasserted. In successive editions of a local paper, the two rival images were reflected in two photographic styles. Both set out, in the manner of the local press, to please their readers and to maintain their circulation by including as many local names and faces as possible. Both aimed to demonstrate to parents the work of their children's schools. They could hardly be more different.

At St David's we do not see learning in progress. Instead, the children greet the camera, their parents and the outside world. They display the products of their learning, holding up certificates and pointing to their paintings. They show their achievements and are themselves achievements. They are the products of a school, presented to the school's customers, their parents. The *process* of learning is private and concealed. The work of expressing the values of the school is done by the certificates, the badges, the tidy uniforms – the

Our School

They've got the whole world in their hands — globe-trotting Joanna Harris and Lucy Warren let their fingers do the walking to far-distant countries on this classroom aid, made by one of their teachers.

Superstars Jonathan Ufton, Alexander Codling, Richard Barwell and John Belsey show off their Amateur Athletics Association Esso awards

The alert and cheerful faces of Form 8F at St David's College.

The work on wildlife goes on show in 7J's classroom.

St David's

Our School

Name has a magic ring

Painting a portrait of his dad — he says — is four-year-old Alan Eldridge.	(V/52546/3)

"Which is the heaviest — the ball, the blackboard brush — or even the teapot?" Scott Havey and Mark Hamblyn ask each other.	(V/52546/18)

Cheering up a playground wall is this animal mural being admired by Leander Boyce, Adam Begbie, Jimmy Nunas, Kenny Palmer.	(V/52546/36)

Boys and girls learn to sew at Merlin. Riki Gilling and Mark Hollidge ply their needles and thread.	(V/52536/10)

An exercise in weights and measures for Malcolm Gray and Erica Dorman, Margaret Lewthwaite and Marcelle Temple.	(V/52536/15)

Merlin

external evidence of learning. In the Merlin pictures we find the familiar image of children absorbed in their work, the process of learning visible in the disposition of their bodies. Here it is the teacher's eye that is represented by the camera and composes the pictures. In the absence of certificates and awards, it is the documentary nature of the picture that reassures parents that learning is taking place.

In the bitter disputes of the 1980s, the interests of 'parents' and 'teachers' were presented as incompatible and irreconcilable. 'Parents' were far less threatened by the St David's type of school, and as we look at these two presentations it is not difficult to understand why. At St David's the teachers appear to have accomplished a task. They have worked on their charges and offered them back to their parents, produced, finished and dealt with. The Merlin pictures, by contrast, make demands on the parents who view them. First they must make an effort to interpret the image – and, more importantly, they are made irrelevant by it. The work of this school is shown not as a service to the parents but as independent development for their children. Child-centred schooling seems to be offering

an unacceptable degree of autonomy to children. Those mechanisms by which the teacher paces and controls the pupil's learning – testing, grading and measuring attainment – seem irrelevant here. Paradoxically, in those pictures where the activities of the children come closest to childlike play, the position of the adult is most under threat. A child at play does not display the subservience which secures adult power. The mistake is to confuse the image of intricate control which characterises the progressive primary classroom with childhood play, which is genuinely self-directed.

The desired image for the right-wing campaigners of the 1980s indicated children's incapacities rather than their capabilities. Perhaps the two most characteristic single images of a child at school are the one with the head bent over a task and the one with the hand raised, eagerly competing for the teacher's attention. The first could be seen as an image of self-motivated learning, but the second acknowledges that this is not altogether desirable. It pulls the child's attention away from his work towards the adult, who will first mediate and then assess. The teacher may not be visible, but the eyes of the eager child gaze towards that potent space and his raised hand

places him in competition with his classmates. This image of the well-adjusted student striving to succeed almost always shows a boy. When testing and grading are all-important, it is not learning but the display of learning, that counts. The aim is to be top of the class.

A controlling image for the concept of excellence in British education has been that of the expensive and prestigious public school and its state-funded imitator, the grammar school, both distinguishable from everyday run-of-the-mill secondary schools by their greater

Two of the schools which featured in the Coventry survey: Headmasters, senior staff and pupils at Alderman Callow (above) and Henry VIII.

company of the majority of my neighbours. Equally, I believe had my parents not been presented with . . . private education for

ment, John Thorn, headmaster of Winchester, echoed these anti-conformist sentiments :—
' Education is full of questi

dozen children to university and

antiquity and more intensive use of ritual and spectacle. Their powerful claim to offer the 'best' education, accompanied by easy access to the 'best' universities and elite professions, has meant that comprehensive schools aiming to offer equal opportunities to all, have been perceived not as an alternative aspiration but as a poor second best. In this view the disappearance of grammar schools meant more than a disappearance of privilege. It meant that 'gifted' children of all classes were to be deprived of an education whose rich traditions were rooted in history. They were abandoned in a comprehensive jungle. When, in the 1980s, changes to the law allowed schools to opt out of local-authority control, or out of the state system altogether, the power of the grammar school image seemed to offer a more attractive alternative.

But the imagery that has given value to newly commodified educational establishments refers further back in history than any other image associated with childhood. It harks back to a pre-industrial world of privilege and to the dignified ranking of a stratified society before the unholy scramble of capitalist exchange and grab. In a future-orientated world of competition, the iconography of traditional schooling embodies a hierarchical past. The signs of a desirable education are still the teacher's gown, the monastic cloister, the Gothic arch. Together they refer us to an ecclesiastical past where learning is associated with godliness, scholarliness is cut off from the mêlée of the everyday world, and the ancient universities cast their magic shade. Above all, they are cut off from political involvement. Perhaps it is not surprising that it is easier to link this mythic image with a market model of education than with a public-service one, for these 'traditions' can be put up for sale. They are very much of the present. The more exotic signifiers of learning have gained economic value as the spectacle of education itself enters the marketplace.

These visual reminders of an elite education bring about an elision between the privileged child and the 'gifted' child. In a metonymic shift, the signs of wealth come to stand for cleverness, those of exclusivity, for excellence. Whenever ordinary, hardworking schools use these devices to represent themselves to their pupils, they are, willy-nilly, recycling the meanings of hierarchy and exclusion. The school uniform in particular can invest its present wearers, with no effort on their part, with a prestige brought by past wearers. The older and more confident the school, the odder its costume and its symbols may be. In recent years even primary schools have returned to compulsory school uniform, as a convenient marker of a proud institution. In its claim to be unchanging, an inheritance from the past, school uniform must be the antithesis of fashion – always out of date, paying no attention to convenience or comfort. To produce your child as a uniform image is to aspire to give them the good things in life, to disguise their Bash Street origins and to secure their upward mobility. The uniform is a sign of contemporary aspiration within an archaic framework.

Uniform is a convenient marker of schooling in other ways. It is a visible sign of the multiplicity characteristic of school imagery and school pupils, and it adds the important ingredient of conformity. It gathers children together in an orderly fashion, gets them literally into line, encourages a uniformity of stance and bodily control as well as dress. It speaks of a uniformity of quality which will transcend individual quirks and oddities. It is a reassuring image for adults, for it tells them where children belong and who is responsible for them. It becomes an easily available shorthand to indicate school itself. The image of conformity, of selection and exclusion, becomes an unavoidable part of the lumber of pedagogical meanings, visually imported even when unwanted. Through uniform, the 'traditional' version of schooling becomes an exemplar of all education.

Shock reports and schools of shame

The image of school appears in the national press in two strikingly different contexts. In the 'quality' press, the *Guardian* education pages and the *Times Education Supplement*, the address is largely to professionals, the type of audience which is conversant with the running of schools and often involved as teachers, governors, or active parents. The imagery is realist and observational, illustrating an argument, exploring a practice. By contrast, in the popular press, images of schooling have increasingly appeared in the context of conflict and outrage. Readers have been told of shock reports and schools of shame. The repertoire of imagery – sometimes visual, sometimes evoked in the rhetoric – creates a soap opera of schools.

In the daily sequencing of the national press, narratives develop over the weeks and years, gaining their own momentum. The 'stories' which propel us forward as we read are not the individual news items but the long-running dramas which provide the framework into which the news is fitted. Built up between the feature pages and the news, the gossip and the pictures, a cast of characters is created, with heroes and villains, victims and aggressors. These roles may be filled by whoever is the subject of the next topical event. Readers follow developments with relish, eager for the next instalment.

Over the 1970s and 1980s, and with increasing acrimony into the 1990s, such a drama built up around education. Its heroes were parents who were at the sharp end of the educational debate and were campaigning for their 'freedom' – the right to choose their

children's schools. The villains were the teachers, determined to thwart the parents and blinded to the children's interests by their devotion to ideology. In this ongoing conflict, children were visible chiefly as the passive by-products of this or that conflicting system. They appeared sometimes alongside angry parents, sometimes deprived of their schooling by militant or incompetent teachers.

The popular papers pose their readers as laypeople, suspicious of teachers who in their view disguise political opinions as professional expertise and use fancy language to deceive and confuse. These readers are likely to be parents with a straightforward, common-sense approach. They may not be well educated themselves, but they are worldly-wise and want the best for their children. They have no stake in perpetuating education as a protected area, for it has been an area from which they have, in any case, been excluded. These are the very parents who have been described as apathetic and uninterested in their children's education. They have seen schools as places of restricted access, from which they have been excluded by arrogant and unaccountable teachers. Such readers will not be surprised when they open their daily papers and peep into the forbidden territory of the school to find dreadful behaviour and scandalous goings-on. Readers are regularly presented with discipline scandals, sexual scandals, and scandals centring on improper teacher behaviour and uncontrollable pupils. Stories explore the margins of schools' activity, unspeakable in professional discourse. When inner-city 'sink' schools, with their almost insuperable problems, hit the headlines, the newspapers took the view that what was needed was more discipline and the higher standards that could be brought about only by 'traditional' teaching methods. Stories about schools were evolved within this framework; actors were typecast; some events were selected, others appeared irrelevant. Education made the front pages when verbal conflict erupted into action – as with the extended dispute over William Tyndale School in the mid 1970s or the teachers' strikes of the mid 1980s. The relatively few pictures of children which accompanied the unfolding drama reflects the secondary place children themselves take in the action, even though the polemic was centrally concerned with the nature of childhood. When children do appear, the 'happiness' of the primary school has changed to a sense of sullen resistance, and schoolchildren's rebelliousness is a narrative theme. Children could legitimately play a part only as pawns in the game or as products of the system. When allowed to speak up for themselves, they demonstrate their own need to be controlled. 'Please sir, don't be trendy', ran a headline in the *Daily Mirror*. The humourless call was for a return to the delightfully ironic three Rs. 'The need to get back to the basics in education – that means the three Rs – is recognised by everyone. Everyone, that is, except the teachers in their ivory classrooms', wrote the *Sun*.

When the Education Reform Act of 1988 introduced a national curriculum and regular assessments for all children at seven, eleven, fourteen and sixteen, the Conservative government could claim that it was in response to public opinion, and particularly the opinions of parents – as expressed in the popular press. The debate continued to rage over the form of the national curriculum, to prevent the progressives from hijacking it for their own ends. A row over the teaching of reading led Education Secretary Kenneth Clarke to describe 'modern' methods as 'cranky'. Children should gain access to the subversive power of the word through graded reading schemes and formal systems rather than through undisciplined access to 'real books'. Knowledge itself must be carefully controlled and designed in such a way that children may be graded, tested and marked for life. A visible disciplinary space is to be reasserted, with the teacher firmly back at the front of the class.

By the beginning of the 1990s, 'the dream of a more egalitarian education had turned into a nightmare'. The traditional image had been triumphantly reasserted, and – deprived of political support, as well as money and equipment – state education itself was seen as second-class, abandoned by all who could afford to do so. A new image was creeping into the pages of the press, an image of crumbling walls and decaying buildings. The *Daily Mirror* ran a

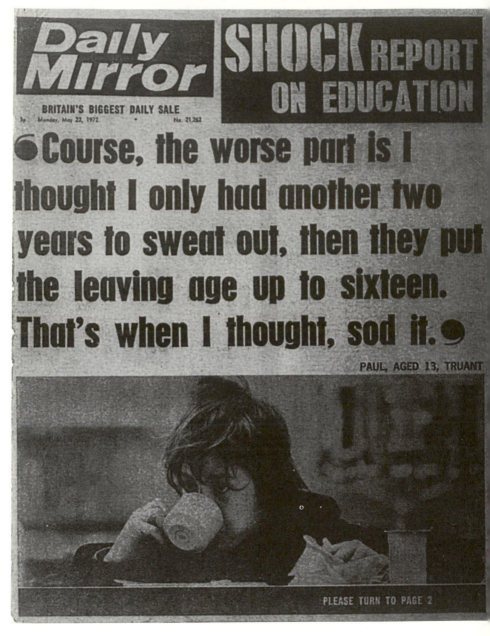

Daily Mirror

BRITAIN'S BIGGEST DAILY SALE

3p   Monday, May 22, 1972   •   No. 21,262

SHOCK REPORT ON EDUCATION

❝Course, the worse part is I thought I only had another two years to sweat out, then they put the leaving age up to sixteen. That's when I thought, sod it.❞

PAUL, AGED 13, TRUANT

PLEASE TURN TO PAGE 2

'Shock report' in 1990, which echoed a similar special issue in 1972. In 1990 the scandal was of inadequate facilities and lack of funds – rooms shared by several classes, outside toilets and leaking roofs. The boy on the front page of 1972 was a school refuser. The school-leaving age had just been raised to sixteen and he couldn't face staying on. The boy on the front page of 1990 wanted to go to school. Now the problem was – there was no room.

4

The fantasy of liberation and the demand for rights

Pictures of children at play in the open spaces of the countryside or city seem like emblems of freedom itself. Here is childhood apparently untrammelled by social restraint. Undirected play, the most childish of activities, expresses everything that envious adults must leave behind.

Melanie Klein described play as the central activity of childhood; 'Play transforms anxiety into pleasure', she wrote. In a Council of Europe publication, clinical psychologist Marie-José Lérés-Richer expanded on Klein's position: 'A child of any age who resorts to play is in a sense entering a private domain – usually secret, magic or sacred – a maintenance area in which every item is taken apart and put together in a genuine process of creation.' The popular image of play tends to seek out the magic but forget the maintenance.

The privacy of children's play tempts the adult eye. The Time-Life book, *Photographing Children* advises the candid photographer simply to wait for 'that magic moment when the movement reveals the child'. Snatching moments from their incessant movement, we grab at those fragile qualities of childhood that are made more poignant by our knowledge – and the children's ignorance – of their imminent loss.

In her book with pictures, *Look at Kids*, Leila Berg developed an eloquent argument for adults to respect children's privacy, to observe but hold back from interfering and imposing good behaviour or formal constraints. She urged them to be humble and learn from what they saw. But pictures of children at play presented purely for adult pleasure may do no more than release the adult from practical responsibility. Unknown and unnamed, placed in no particular relationship to the pictured child, viewers may react as they please.

FORUM
COUNCIL OF EUROPE

CONTENTS

MAKE RIGHTS A REALITY

THE CHILD

CHILDREN'S RIGHTS

THE CHILDREN ACT

■ Proceedings for interim care or supervision orders

The powers of the court to make interim orders are substantially changed by the Act. The provisions of section 38 which authorise their making apply:

a) in any adjourned proceedings on an application for a care or supervision order;

b) where the court gives a direction under section 37 which empowers the court to direct the local authority to investigate the child's circumstances in any family proceedings;

c) where the court in proceedings on an application for care or supervision order, makes a residence order instead – unless it is satisfied that the child's welfare will be satisfactorily safeguarded [section 38(3)].

On making an interim care order or supervision order the court may give such directions as it considers appropriate for a medical or psychiatric examination or other assessment of the child. But if the child is of sufficient understanding to make an informed decision, she may refuse to submit to the examination or other assessment [section 38(6)].

The court cannot make an interim care order or supervision order unless satisfied that there are reasonable grounds for believing that the circumstances for making a full order exist.

Unless the Act specifies otherwise, interim orders have the same effect as full orders. As...

■ Wardship

Section 7 of the Family Law Reform Act 1969 ceases to have effect so that it is no longer possible for local authorities to use the High Court's inherent jurisdiction to place a child...

This way the Act ensures that local authorities cannot circumvent the grounds for emergency protection or care or supervision orders.

In any case, many of the advantages hitherto associated with wardship, particularly in relation to kinds of evidence are transferred to...

A care or supervision order may be discharged or varied by the court on the application of:
a) anyone who has parental responsibility for the child;
b) the child himself;
c) the local authority.

This image is free-floating; viewers are not addressed as parents, teachers or caring professionals. Unanchored in our everyday lives, it makes no demands on us, presents us with no challenge. Apparently outside structured social relationships, these pictures are the most susceptible to adult fantasy.

The imagery associated with campaigns for children's rights must negotiate a tension between a compelling adult fantasy of liberation and the far from liberatory actuality of children's lives. Attempts to match the freedom of the image with an equivalent freedom in the world runs up against contradictory perspectives. It may be that children's liberation is an impossible dream, an adult longing to re-create a past that never was; or the problem may be seen as the corrupting influence of contemporary life itself, depriving children of their childhood. Children's liberation movements – at the turn of the century, in the 1920s and again in the 1970s – have sought to face these contradictions and test the fantasy against everyday reality. If this involves negotiating a public space for the voices of children themselves, it may well produce writing and pictures which are far removed from the magic moments sought by candid photographers. The mundane facts of children's everyday experience have meant that liberatory aspirations are uneasily linked with the demand for rights. The one keeps children outside cultural constraints; the other insists that they enter on comparable terms to adults.

The first Declaration of the Rights of the Child was drafted in 1924 by Eglantyne Jebb, founder of the Save the Children International Fund: 'The whole world stands to gain if children grow up strong and healthy, able and willing to work for the good of their fellow men. For better or worse, the world can be revolutionised in one generation according to how we deal with the children.' Yet an international commitment to children's rights has taken the best part of a century to achieve. In 1959 came the United Nations Declaration of the Rights of the Child, in the form of ten succinct principles. Its preamble affirmed: 'Mankind owes the child the best it has to give.' Twenty years later, in 1979, the International Year of the Child was declared. But a further ten years passed, and many negotiations were conducted, before the General Assembly of the United Nations adopted the Convention on the Rights of the Child. By the early 1990s many member states, including the United States and Britain, had still to ratify it, since their laws remained incompatible with some of its terms.

The 1959 Declaration and the 1989 Convention recognised the powerlessness of children and their need for protection to ensure their right to survive, grow and be healthy, cared for and educated, and to remain free from neglect, torture, physical, sexual or mental abuse. In the 1989 Convention these survival, development and protection rights were joined by a new set of participation rights: children have the right to express opinions and have those opinions taken into account; to exercise freedom of thought, conscience and religion; to meet with others and form associations, and to have access to and share information. The Convention expressly commits signatories to make its provisions widely known to children in a language which they, as well as adults, can understand.

In Britain in the 1970s a vigorous campaign for children's rights went well beyond these modest claims for respect and dignity. The children's liberation movement laid a claim for children's autonomy even at the expense of their protection. Children should not be satisfied with taking their place as junior partners in an adult society, it claimed. Given their freedom, they could revolutionise that society. 'The first duty of a revolutionary is to build a society geared to children' was the slogan that introduced the first five issues of *Children's Rights* magazine, launched in 1971. In its short and controversial existence it attempted to hold together a heady call for social and sexual revolution with a re-evaluation of the nature of childhood itself. This project nearly ended in disaster when the magazine produced a 'Bust Book' which advised children to fight the police and resist arrest. It was rescued by its eminent board of advisers, including A.S. Neill and Leila Berg, who sacked the editor and relaunched it under a new title, *Kids*. They made it clear that the fatal mistake had been for adult editors to attempt to speak from the position of children. 'If the Bust Book article had been written by a group of kids,' wrote Leila Berg, ' . . . it would not have been taken as a "practical guide" but as a demand to have attention paid.'

The dangers inherent in an inappropriate confusion between adult and child shadowed the children's liberation movement. But writings in the 'alternative' magazines of the time argued that the boundaries between adults and children must be readjusted despite the risks. Only then could society be both more free and more rational. If adults desired the playfulness of childhood, children should be granted the privileges of adulthood. It was a plea not to protect an endangered childhood but to escape from childhood altogether.

The movement had its own critical and theoretical writings. The influential Penguin Education imprint published British editions of books already well known in the United States, from Everett Reimer's *School is Dead* to John Holt's *Escape from Childhood*. It rediscovered a history which began with the experimental schools and the sexual radical movements at the turn of the century and continued into the present with A.S. Neill's Summerhill. Founded in 1926, Summerhill was 'that dreadful school' where children were left to make their own choices, including the decision on whether to attend lessons or simply to rush about in gangs, expressing what Neill, in his numerous books, described as childhood 'savagery'. Experiments of the early 1970s, both inside and outside the state system, included free schools on the Summerhill model, and innovations like truancy centres which provided for school refusers who would otherwise be hanging around on the streets, learning exchanges, 'schoolkids'' unions, radical teachers' groups, and campaigners who aimed, in the words of Ivan Illich, to 'deschool society' and reject the strictures of institutions altogether. The movement had an international awareness through the writings of Illich, based in Mexico, and Paulo Freire, who worked in the slums of Rio. The oppression of children in the Third World was a prominent theme.

This new climate of debate made it acceptable to explore the feelings of frustration and helplessness experienced by many children particularly at school. A 'new' sociology of education took schoolchildren's daily experience seriously, and expanded curricula in the teachers' training colleges included radical critiques of the school system and dealt with such topics as pupil perceptions of school and school resistance. The new climate gave some children the opportunity to express complaints openly. Insubordination could be unashamed, seen as the resistance of an unjustly repressed group.

'All over the world school has an anti-educational effect on children', wrote Keith Paton in his pamphlet *The Great Brain Robbery*, a critique of the orthodox philosophy of education. The argument was that schools were not enabling but limiting. They shut off avenues of exploration rather than opening them up and erected artificial divisions between adults and children. Radical teachers who wanted to change this state of affairs and explore more collaborative ways of learning faced a dilemma of self-definition: 'The most immediate contradiction we've got to face is how to be ourselves in the classroom, how to free ourselves (and hence the kids) from the idea of "the teacher".' For others the answer was 'alternative' schools, in which children would be participants as well as pupils. The White Lion Free School in London, one of the more long-lasting and articulate, aimed to break down many different kinds of boundaries – between holiday and term, between pupils and teachers, between teachers and other adults who worked in the school, between teachers and parents and between teachers and the world beyond. A commitment to children's rights in education meant that childhood was to be a positive value once more. Children should be allowed to evolve their own forms of expression, and not be channelled into those already laid down by the adult world.

The pictures of child-centred education current at the time were not pictures in which radical teachers or school students could recognise themselves. There was a yawning gap between those calm and orderly photographs of the progressive classroom and the helpless, chaotic experience of school expressed in the 'schoolkids'' magazines and those produced by some young teachers' groups. The

school system was shown as mechanical and inflexible, directed towards a future that was equally limited. Individuals were reduced to mere items, crumbs from a mincing machine. School itself was shown as imprisonment, or as brutal mental or physical suppression. 'Schools imprison your mind and control your body . . . they don't encourage us to develop our potential but rather tame our natural inclinations, causing total apathy in most and rebellion in very few', wrote the school student editors of *Braindamage*.

The imagery of escape, both mental and physical, gave the magazines produced by the few rebellious pupils in the mid 1970s a sense of euphoria and vigour. They had names like *Braindamage, Fang, Miscarriage* (produced in Hackney) and *Blazer* – and were short-lived. They shared a sense of urgency and drama. Whatever their quality, their very existence was a challenge, an assertion of pupils' right to address each other publicly and to speak aloud those things which are normally giggled over or muttered. Informal school culture became public.

These magazines did not reject school, but demanded 'schools not prisons'. However, their conviction that their approach was reasonable was tempered with an awareness that any appeal to reason must be constantly renegotiated, for schoolchildren's demands are unlikely to be taken seriously by arbitrary and irrational authority. The pupils saw themselves as reasonable, but knew that in the eyes of the authorities this was an empty claim. They constantly returned to a sense of deep injustice and impotent outrage when adult action failed to match adult rhetoric. The magazines published a stream of letters and anecdotes describing routine humiliations and patient, 'reasonable' requests which had come to nothing. 'Have you ever been ticked off for bringing a paper carrier bag to school for your books because it is inappropriate or not strong enough?' wrote Skinners' School third-year pupils. 'Sometimes when you're at a table you're not allowed to speak, but why can grown-ups speak?' asked Karen, aged ten, both in *Children's Rights 2*.

Apparently trivial demands like regulated length of hair and the wearing of uniform gained enormous significance as the centre of symbolic battles. As children, these writers found that irrationality was expected of them. They were trapped by the way they were defined. In turn they embraced irrationality as an appropriate expression of their situation. Irrational fury and rational solutions were presented together in a chaotic visual style. There was a need for an imagery that would both represent children to each other and at the same time deny adults the fullness of that representation. Hence the tendency to antagonise and shock. 'The impossible generation bites deeper', declared *Miscarriage*. With bad spelling, scribbled drawings and disorderly pages, adults' view of children

LIBERTARIAN EDUCATION 11

formerly Libertarian Teacher

12 P

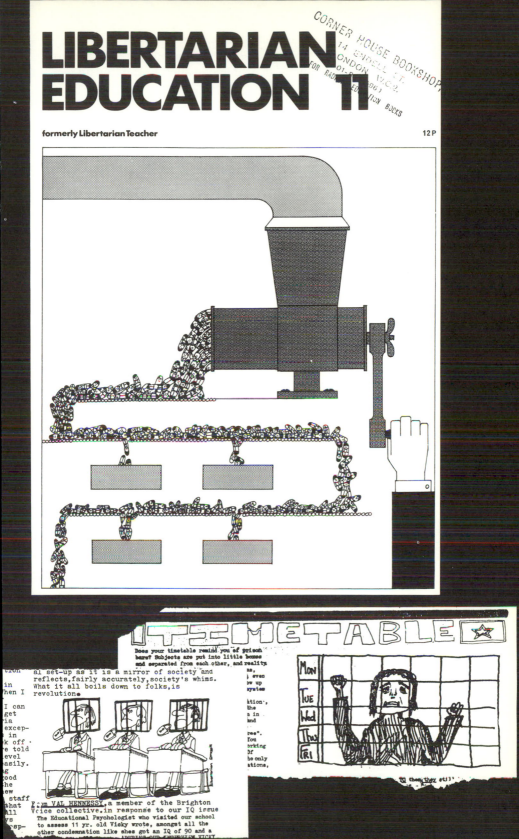

TIMETABLE ☆

Does your timetable remind you of prison
bars? Subjects are put into little boxes
and separated from each other, and reality

al set-up as it is a mirror of society and
reflects, fairly accurately, society's whims.
What it all boils down to folks, is
revolution

From VAL HENNESSY, a member of the Brighton
Voice collective, in response to our IQ issue
The Educational Psychologist who visited our school
to assess 11 yr. old Vicky wrote, amongst all the
other condemnation like shes got an IQ of 90 and a

was thrown back at them. The magazines drew on the language of the student movement and the proletarian image of the clenched fist, the dream imagery of hippiedom, but above all, the anarchic imagery of children's comics.

Comics are traditionally complicit with children's interests. Their prices are low so that they can be bought with pocket money, and on the whole they are free from educational overtones. They are frowned upon by adults and forbidden in class. Their inventiveness and irreverence remain icons of children's refusal to be shaped into an image acceptable to adults. Dennis the Menace and the Bash Street kids have come closer to expressing children's experience of childhood and school than any more respectable medium. They started their disruptive careers in the 1950s and have kept their appeal into the 1990s, successfully competing with newer inventions. 'A menace never changes', declared Dennis in March 1991, refusing to be

updated with tracksuit and personal stereo. Instead, the characters in *Beano* and *Dandy* remain close to the spirit of the tramps and messenger boys in the very first comics of the 1890s, inhabiting a world that is unequivocally working-class and urban. Their one aim remains to outsmart adults and teachers. In Bash Street, the long-suffering teacher with his mortarboard and swishing cane has himself hardly changed over a hundred years of comics.

Comic-book kids take perverse pleasure in an image of childhood which rejects any form of attractiveness. The Bash Street Gang are weedy, ugly or oddball. They are mostly boys, but Beryl the Peril and Minnie the Minx are in the same mould. They are reverse exhibitionists. In drawing attention to an unacceptable surface, they reject adult sympathy and attempts at understanding. Their appearance is designed to repel. Their chosen image erects an antagonising shield of ugliness which may keep selfhood secret within it.

In the spirit of the comic book, the gaze of the adult may be met head on with a challenging glare – and this is the image that was taken up by the children's liberation movement for the cover of books and magazines. The experience of betrayal is in the simmering aggression of the stare. The contempt in the eyes of the girl from the Third World, the calculating gaze of the boy on the cover of *Children's Rights*, are looks that refuse deference, that recognise but defy the demand for acquiescence. These children are shown as people who – in the words of Paul Adams in a collection of essays, *Children's Rights* – have the right to live in a meaningful world and to have a moral sense, but instead are offered opportunism, expediency, absurdity and non-participation. The look from these front pages is not an innocent one. It claims the right to express anger and refuses any sense of guilt. Even the injunction to look at kids in a generous and empathetic way becomes uneasy when children claim the right to look back. The concept of liberation poses a dilemma of power and control which is more acute for those adults who support its claims than for those more repressive adults to whom it directs its challenge. For this image is an anti-humanist one. It does its best to reject the comforting assumption of a shared common humanity which can all too easily be taken and exploited.

Writers like John Holt have insisted that children are not different from adults – or at least, not different in the ways that are commonly assumed. They are not less conscious of their rights, or less sensitive to disrespectful treatment. Nor are they less able to assess a situation and make coherent decisions on their actions. Yet out of this claim, another form of difference can emerge. A neo-Romantic view of childhood places children outside a sick society which itself does not respect human values. 'How can human beings emerge in a society that has such rampant nihilism as does ours? Where all values are discredited and unmasked? Where the order of the day is opportunism, expediency, action rooted in no ethical judgement? Where people grow up immersed in anomie, aloofness, relativity, absurdity, indefiniteness and non-participation?' asked Paul Adams.

In this view it is children, rather than the adults who claim to train them, who should be seen as the keepers of true values – particularly those values of community, rationality and sexuality without guilt that adult society has lost. Adults should be learning from children, not the other way round. If childlike values were allowed to develop freely, we would stand a better chance of achieving a future of peace, co-operation and harmony. The call for self-regulation is in part a desire for children to develop free from the anti-human qualities of society itself. 'Surely it is central to our beliefs that if a child's natural impulses are not suppressed he will become social and self-regulated *without compulsion*', wrote Keith Paton in *Kids*. 'That is, he will satisfy his needs without greed or acquisitiveness, will learn easily if and when he is interested and will be *genuinely* co-operative and considerate to others.' Children are owed a better society, but at the same time they are asked to create a better society on our behalf.

A nostalgia for a possible harmonious childhood merged easily with a nostalgia for the mythic harmony of society itself, a time when

the social group was small and cohesive, when children and adults did meaningful work together that was not strenuous or exploitative and learning happened, incidentally, along the way. The setting up of rural communes where adults brought up children together was an attempt to recapture that simple spirit. The aim of creating an 'organic community' – Paul Goodman's phrase – lay behind much of the free-school thinking, but their intention was to root the school in an existing inner-city community. Their nostalgia was for the imagined cohesion of the urban working class rather than that of the rural peasant. The free-school movement insisted that an appropriate space for learning should refuse traditional demarcations. Schools should not be the peaceful oases envisaged by Plowden, but should be open to the surrounding world. The streets should be seen not as a place of danger and corruption, but as potential learning opportunities. Children should be free to wander where they will, invading adult territory, entering places of work, exploring and asking questions. 'There are plenty of learning situations outside, and there could be more if workers inside assisted in a mass jail break and turned their energies into making society more educative for everyone, not just kids,' wrote Keith Paton. Learning should take precedence over economic activity, and the values of childhood should permeate society.

Pictures in books in the 1970s such as Colin Ward's *The Child and the City* captured the last moments before road and office redevelopment transformed the British urban landscape. They show children amongst piles of rubble, hiding in disused buildings and

TRUANCY CENTRE

The Children had already taken over this derelict factory in North London. It had been empty for three years, bought by the

for eight children. (She's a 'registered mother' registered with the local health authorities as an approved child minder. She

writing with chalk on the paving stones. Free schools and truancy centres were themselves often in squatted warehouses or other empty buildings. The indulgent adult's desire not to interfere is strongly tested as children take risks with fire, piles of rubble and abandoned machinery, moving at the edge of danger. The self-conscious realism of this urban imagery sought to reject the moralism and Romanticism which linked children with the rural and with organic nature, but in treating the town as a space for discovery it created its own urban ruralism. Children were not expected to invade the centres of modernity and power. Instead they sought out quaint customs and craftspeople at work. They looked for elderly characters with a tale to tell. The hiding places, nooks and crannies of the inner city were for all the world like the lanes and copses of the countryside. This imagery set its face against the hardness and glitter of the new city in a nostalgia for the manipulability of the old.

The political aspects of the children's liberation movement ranged fron the vanguardist Schools Action Union – 'SAU is working to build a militant, self-disciplined national organisation dedicated to struggling for day-to-day democratic control of the schools . . .' – to a broadly based campaign for participation rights. But to the popular press children's politics meant, and has continued to mean, unruly street demonstrations organised by 'Schoolkid Castros' incited by subversive teachers. Only the cane would be appropriate discipline for such riotous behaviour. But the mundane image of the democratic meeting had long played an important part in the challenge to unequal relations between adults and children. Decision-making at A.S. Neill's Summerhill was by school meeting, where – in theory at least – no one's voice should count for more than anyone else's, regardless of age or position.

The 1979 United Nations Year of the Child brought the opportunity to publicise definitions of children's rights which moved beyond protection to participation. The Advisory Centre for Education published a draft Charter of Children's Rights, which was grudgingly welcomed by the 'schoolkids'' magazine *Miscarriage*, which described ACE as a 'mild, liberal group of people'. The Charter concluded: 'Children's rights are no different in nature, nor do they demand any different interpretation than is applied to the rights of adults.' In 1986 Robert Franklin, editor of a new collection of essays, *The Rights of Children*, put a similar argument around a claim that children should have the right to vote. 'Arguments in favour of child suffrage have too frequently been ridiculed rather than met,' he wrote. But 'that position is a clear violation of the principle that no individual or group should be subject to laws which they have not participated in making.' Pictures which accompany such arguments are sober, without the excessive qualities of childhood. They are far

Most of the schools organise their own hustings effectively enough at every general election.

X marks the spot for the children

All manner of arguments used to be put forward against giving women the vote. Equally illogical, suggests Bob Franklin, is the contemporary refusal to think of enfranchising our children.

CHILDREN'S lack of political rights, especially the right to vote or be members of political parties, makes them a unique group in democracies. Their position is a while those without property proved their inability to direct their affairs by their very lack of property; a similar circularity of "logic" excluded slaves and black thought and do make informed choices, from decisions about which television programme to watch or which football team to support, to strategies for hand- not children, to make mistakes is hypocrisy. Why not allow children to learn from mistakes and so grow in experience and knowledge? tence and not age, then it is not children who should be excluded but the incompetence. Such a position would exclude as many adults as children and lead to any, interest in poli would probably abstain. Children do possess skills necessary to vote

less gratifying to adult fantasies than more engaging images of childhood, for they deprive the viewer both of the heady opportunity to identify with a liberatory childishness and of the equally gratifying opportunity for violent denunciation.

By the 1980s the campaign for children's rights had made definite changes to public perceptions of childhood, although arguments for children's liberation had come to seem hopelessly romantic and outmoded. The alternative-education projects and small-circulation magazines closed down, no longer viable owing to lack of funds and the changing political climate. Children's voices had gained some legitimacy. The 1975 Children Act had begun to shift the balance of legal rights between parents and children – until then, the law had regarded them as a single entity. Long-standing organisations in the field of child protection and child welfare sought to produce images of childhood that would reflect the change. The concern, however, was to protect the family against state intervention, and the 1989 Children Act raised the threshold for such intervention. The role-reversal posters produced by Saatchi and Saatchi for the NSPCC in 1989 placed undersized parents on the laps of oversized children. They made the point without either an appeal outside the family or the risk of a dangerous confusion between adult and child.

96

Sit down and have a long listen to your kids.

NSPCC

Most strikingly, with the growing public awareness of international issues, the pressure for children's rights has evolved a global, multicultural imagery. Posters from UNICEF publicising the 1989 Convention show not the glowering directness of the 1970s liberation movement, but a cheerful multiplicity. The Convention recognises that children have a right to their own cultural customs and values, and the presentations reflect this diversity of skin colour and costume. But the balance between the support of cultural difference and the claim to universal rights is a delicate one, particularly in the case of girl children, whose disadvantage is often fundamental to a sense of cultural identity. In 1990 UNICEF gave a 'priority focus' to

CHILDREN'S R

UNICEF–UK
55 Lincoln's Inn Fields,
London WC2A 3NB

the girl child, with a view to eliminating gender disparity, particularly in nutrition, health and education. The aim is for a recognition of differences that do not lead to conflict, but this is precisely where the image of childhood runs up against its limits. Childhood is sought as that space beyond conflict, before those rigid differences have taken hold, as a point where 'humanity' aspires to an impossible escape from 'society'. But children live out their lives structured by the imperatives of culture, gender and language. An effective demand for children's rights can take place only within these structures.

HTS

THE CONVENTION ON THE RIGHTS OF THE CHILD

gives legal force to the human rights of every child, regardless of race, colour, sex, disability, national, ethnic or social background, or economic circumstance.

Children's rights can be grouped in four essential categories:

SURVIVAL
Every child has a right to nourishing food, clean water and effective health care.

DEVELOPMENT
Every child has a right to develop to his or her full potential, loved, cared for, and afforded every opportunity to learn and to play.

PROTECTION
Every child has a right to protection from war and from any form of violence, from mental, physical and sexual abuse, from exploitative work and abandonment.

PARTICIPATION
Every child has a right to a name and nationality, a right to have his or her opinions taken into account, and a right to participate, more fully with increasing maturity, in all the activities of society.

"Adherence to, or breach of, the Convention on the Rights of the Child should rapidly become a matter of national concern, of national pride or of national shame."

UNICEF *The State of the World's Children*

UNICEF ⊛ UK

5
No future:
The impossibility of youth

'Everyone was having a pleasant morning here. Mums and Dads were sitting outside with their children enjoying the sunshine when these hooligans started running all over the place. It frightened everybody', reported the *Daily Express* of a 'Day trip to terror'. On that Bank Holiday afternoon in 1980, children who were sitting peacefully with their families were terrified by people at the limits of childhood, 'young troublemakers' who had escaped parental control and started running all over the place.

As young people – teenagers, adolescents, young adults; no single description seems adequate – have asserted themselves with increasing visibility, it has fallen to the national press on the one hand and the advertising industry on the other to define the meaning of 'youth' and to circulate ideas that will quell the unease aroused by these awkward individuals. The press has responded to the ever-changing parade of youth cultures and outrageous behaviour sometimes with amusement, sometimes with horror, always with trepidation. The advertising industry, on the other hand, had encouraged a consolidation of a lucrative target group. Market research from Mark Abrams's *The Teenage Consumer* of 1959, which noted the spending power of postwar youngsters and established a new consumer category, to Gold Greenlees Trott's *Spoilt Brats* of 1990, selling to young people had meant finding out who they think they are and analysing their tastes and attitudes. But although youth styles have ranged from the outlandish to the hyperconformist, their changeability and inventiveness have not necessarily been on the market's terms. Conspicuous display has often been at odds with

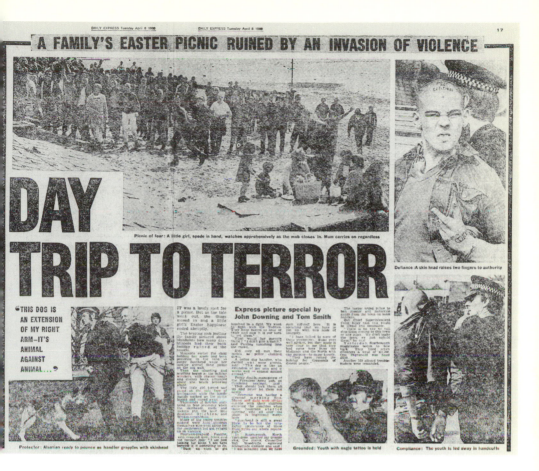

A FAMILY'S EASTER PICNIC RUINED BY AN INVASION OF VIOLENCE

DAY TRIP TO TERROR

Picnic of fear: A little girl, spade in hand, watches apprehensively as the mob closes in. Mum carries on regardless

Defiance :A skin head raises two fingers to authority

THIS DOG IS AN EXTENSION OF MY RIGHT ARM—IT'S ANIMAL AGAINST ANIMAL...

Express picture special by John Downing and Tom Smith

Protector: Alsatian ready to pounce as handler grapples with skinhead

Grounded: Youth with eagle tattoo is held

Compliance: The youth is led away in handcuffs

high consumer expenditure, and so has become a site of contest. For 'youth' also became seen as a time of escape from family ties and social conventions. Over the years, no sooner have we been told that the young are settling down, putting student unrest and rebellious permissiveness behind them, than the reassuring picture has collapsed and a different sort of moral panic has ensued. In 1988 an article in *Campaign* claimed that 'Thatcher's youth' were becoming caring and family-orientated, their aspirations centring on designer clothes, a successful career and a flashy car. But by 1990, these affluent conformists had become 'spoilt brats'. 'Your son is 15. He lost his virginity two years ago, swills Carlsberg Special Brew and slouches in front of the television watching EastEnders,' wrote Rufus Olins in the *Observer*. By 1991, street riots and teenage joy-riding in stolen cars had hit the front pages.

Children in their mid teens are shown as a noisy and disruptive presence in the well-furnished home, but the real problem comes

DON'T BLAME US!

MARTIN: not free enough.

MICHELE: wasting time.

I'll go on the Pill at 16 in case..

MICHELE BISSELL, 15, from Kentish Town, London:

● MUM'S a real hypocrite. She can shout and swear but when we say what we think, or swear, we are treating her like dirt.

If I don't agree with someone, I think I ought to tell them rather than be trampled on and hate it secretly.

If I had my way I would have already left school. I hate it. I'm wasting my time doing things other people want.

If I went out with a guy and wanted sex, I would, I don't want that sort of thing now. I will go on the Pill when I'm 16, just in case. Mum says sleeping around makes you a slut. That's what she thinks, I don't.

Older people say put us in the Army. That's just so someone else will be telling us what to do. You must go through life and make your own mistakes. Why can't we learn for ourselves?

I accept that we all have to tidy up and help at home.

Mum says she pays for the house so she tells us what to do. Well, I think that's wrong. It's our house. We all live here.

School was a bore

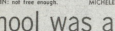

MARTIN, 15, from East Finchley, London:

● School was a bore and I wasn't learning much. They treated you like kids, not free enough. I didn't like being told what to do, so I started bunking off at about 14. Now I've got a job and I'm much happier.

When I was younger my dad belted me, but I don't think it was a bad thing — it helped me change.

Dad nearly killed me when he caught me sniffing glue, and I'm glad now because I know it can lead to other things like drugs.

[A keen Spurs supporter, Martin was jumped on at a game in Manchester and kicked by a group of United supporters. He says he has given aggro to rival supporters near his home ground.] When a fight starts you just get carried away. Throw a brick — it just seems like a good laugh at the time. You don't really think of hurting somebody.

The younger generation is violent. I don't know why. But it has nothing to do with the telly. I can tell you that.

Now I steer clear of trouble. My attitudes have changed since I started working.

GIRLS ARE A BIG PROBLEM

DAVID SULLIVAN, 14, from Aldershot, Hants:

● It's usually girls who cause trouble. At school if there is a fight going on, nine times out of ten it's girls—kicking, scratching, biting and pulling each other's hair.

GEOFF SCANLON (left) and FREDDIE CLERK: all the kids smash things.

when they abandon the cosy living-room and take to the streets. The brick wall behind young Geoff and Freddie in the presentation from a 1977 *Daily Mirror*, like many other brick walls associated with working-class young people, indicates an inner-city wasteland where the 'young savages' may run free. 'These young savages emerge as iron-hard, unfeeling boys and girls without any sense of moral values or sexual values, without any ambition or desire to be worthwhile citizens or to be part of a decent society', wrote Marje Proops. She accompanied her judgement with a lashing attack on parents: 'Mothers who "have a bit on the side", fathers who "fancy a nice bit of skirt" and frequently indulge their fancy, do not keep secret from their offspring their extra-marital activities. Why, therefore, should children, reared in amorality, regard sex as anything more than animal coupling?' In a characteristic reluctance to attribute autonomous decisions to children – even teenagers – writers have regularly blamed parents. 'The children of the 90s will be the children of the "divorce cynics" . . . one in three young adults will come from broken families; many others will have their adolescence disrupted by rows between parents that make life a misery,' reported Rufus Olins in 1990. The consequence will be a generation of children 'more screwed up than any generation before them'.

SUNDAY BEST   Woman's world   EDITED BY UNITY HALL

PROUD OF A PUNK

His hair is crazy but mum thinks he's lovely

PROUD DAD: "She's got a lot of guts and I admire her"

DAD HOPES IT'S A PHASE

WHEN you pass punks in the street, do you wonder how on earth their mums and dads let them go out looking like that?

To the rest of us, punks look weird and tough, but what do their parents think? Are they really as horrible as they appear?

The answer, according to the parents we talked to, is a firm no. Underneath those mad Mohican hair-dos, startling make-up and way-out clothes are typical teenagers.

As I talked to Norma Wilson, a slim, 39-year-old receptionist, her 18-year-old son Lloyd, with his Mohican dyed a brilliant blue, offered to make a cup of tea.

The sight of this tough-looking boy in his heavy black boots and spiky leather bracelets making the tea was, to put it mildly, a surprise.

"Lloyd thinks nothing of doing a few chores," said her mum. "He's a good boy.

"Now he's not working he vacuums the place for me and will do the washing up. We get on very well."

Lloyd was quick to point out he did not lose his job because of his haircut.

SACKED

"I was a packer and when the cleaner left the ...

By HEATHER KIRBY

another job anyway. Said his mum. "When ... told me he was ... have a Mohican ... 'Don't you dare ... couple of days ... it was. What ...

"Now I'm us ... he is the sam ... and helpful.

"He hogs ... he can see ... ing in my ... mirror, b ... in affairs ...

PROUD MUM: "He's a good boy—polite and helpful"

light on his choice of style. "I just like it," he said simply.

"It's not because I'm rebellious or aggressive ...

lacked. People say he's asking for trouble dressing the way he does, but I don't see why.

"Just because he likes ...

THE contrast between Keith Overington, a 43-year-old middle-class ...wager, and his 15-...daughter ...

...goes, I look at it this way at least it's new and unique, I'd feel far worse she wore raggedy ...clothes."

...in the sitting room, Mrs Overington refused to come out of the kitchen.

"She's ashamed of me." said Claire. "She won't ...

The aim is to recapture disaffected young people for childhood, and reduce their challenge to mere bravado. A father may be 'Proud of a punk', as he was in the *News of the World* presentation, even though she wears a T-shirt that proclaims there's 'No future'. Since fathers' futures are conventionally expressed through their children, the denial of that future introduces bizarre contradictions into a presentation that seeks to demonstrate that, despite all, tearaway children can still be contained by their families. Those who refuse such containment may get into the inside pages as runaways, children who have disappeared from their homes – often, inexplicably, 'good' homes – and taken to the free spaces of the streets. There they face possible degradation and come under the control of a new set of social agents with the right to define them. Most conspicuous amongst these are the police, whose claim 'We control the streets' is enforced by violence when necessary, and whose definitions may be crude. 'The dog is an extension of my right arm,' one police officer told the *Daily Express*. 'It's animal against animal.'

The softer agencies – social services, youth training, further education – aim to entice young people into schemes that will bridge the gap between the abandoned disciplines of childhood and the yet unestablished disciplines of adulthood. But the lure of the streets has remained. With the first youth cults of the 1950s, when the Teddy Boys, in their sharp expensive suits, their greasy hairdos and their assertive ways, fascinated and frightened the respectable populace, an imagery of glitter and decay accompanied the attractions and moral ambiguity of their exploration of public places. The neon and pinball machines of a seedy night life complemented the street corners and the crumbling estates. By the late 1980s city centres had lost their hospitable face. Young people who had rejected the values of home and escaped from the social agencies designed to contain them were now found sleeping in shop doorways covered only in blankets and cardboard. Despite the increase in youth affluence, the glitter and decay of the 1950s have been replaced by the clubland and cardboard city of the 1990s. Yet despite the dangers, the theme of escape retains its attraction, for unlike the fantasies of childhood, in the imagery of youth we glimpse a possible life outside the constraints of society.

The public imagery of childhood tends to take itself for granted. It rarely reflects or comments on its own construction. Not so with the imagery of youth. 'Youth' has regularly made the front pages of the popular press. Special editions of newspapers are devoted to it. It makes up both the readership and the topic of magazines on style, fashion and music. The characteristics of youth have been endlessly nagged over and studied. Images of youth have been examined and dissected, catalogued and discussed, as if the image itself could give some clue to the nature of this elusive phenomenon. In a system of meanings which creates rigid categorical differences, 'youth' must be a non-category, nothing but the dividing line between two well-defined types. Hovering problematically on the margins of both, it is pulled first in one direction, then in the other. The indications of childhood are no longer appropriate, and those of adulthood are withheld or refused. When teenagers appear, the categories of child and adult themselves seem uncertain and fluctuating. And so we have the paradox whereby these people who should logically be absent, since they hardly exist, are in fact the most strikingly present in the media and in public imagery. Again and again we are invited to scrutinise them and consider the puzzle of their non-identity. One way of understanding the turbulent imagery of youth is to see it as a set of strategies for coping with this impossible group and its

STRAIGHTS! PUNKS! MODS! SKINHEADS!

LOUNGING: Newcastle mods idle hours away.   REBELLING: Skinhead look, with cobwebs.

KIDS! Just look at them. Rings through their noses, hair like porcupines. Men with earrings, girls in big boots.

Bloody kids! Who do they think they are?

In an extraordinary series of interviews and pictures, the Mirror takes a unique look at the teenagers of Britain today.

They talk about everything. Sex, money, parents, music—even how often they have a bath. There has never been anything quite like it before.

You may think you know what kids are like. But do you?

Keith Waterhouse's astonishing report begins tomorrow. Sometimes raw and shocking. Sometimes funny and outrageous. Sometimes sad and touching.

SWINGING: A student shops in Liverpool.   Bloody kids! In the Mirror tomorrow.   HAIR-RAISING: A punk girl parades in King's Road, Chelsea.

: School break—and there's time for a kiss and cuddle.

Bloody kids! WHO DO THEY THINK THEY ARE? FIND OUT STARTING IN THE MIRROR TOMORROW

possible freedoms. The theme of 'No future' can both be cataclysmic and point to an eternal present.

From the late 1970s to the mid 1980s the imagery was prolific. 'Youth', it appeared, had not one manifestation but many. Newspapers provided their readers with visual inventories in which strange exotic types were identified, their characteristics analysed, their tastes in music and dance noted, their lifestyles distinguished each from the others. The tone ranged from pleasurable amazement to something just short of moral outrage. 'Kids, just look at them. Rings through their noses, hair like porcupines. Men with earrings, girls in boots. Bloody kids! Who do they think they are?' exclaimed the *Daily Mirror* in April 1983.

This was an exercise in decoding, a search for an understanding of youth itself through a reading of the signs – the tattooed cobweb, the spiked hair, the boots and braces. There was a wealth of detail, every item claiming significance. Sometimes they were catalogued by diagrams, but more often photography was used to record and pin

down, in a series of frozen moments, the ever-changing language of youth. The pictures offered the rich and pleasurable surface of fashion photography, responding to the spectacular values presented by their subjects. They drew out the drama and wit of the costume, aiming to entertain. The hunt was on for the weirdest of the weirdies and the craziest of the head-bangers. The jangling of different styles offers a pleasure Roland Barthes described as 'babel', a carnivalesque space where incoherence can momentarily be indulged. We can gasp with amazement or laugh at their sheer cheek, for this imagery is not at the expense of its subjects. We are aware of a collaboration, if an uneasy one, between performers and presenters. Growth out of the childhood involves a challenge to the adult's unlimited right to look and an unwillingness to accept the controlling gaze. And yet here they are, forcing themselves into view, demanding the attention of the lens. As they become aware of our gaze and its power they engage in a visible negotiation with it, presenting themselves ready-made, *as* an image. It may be an image designed to amuse, or it may be one which aims to alienate the viewer, meeting adult indulgence with adolescent contempt, in a search for those signs that will shock the most. Punk took these tendencies to the extreme with its safety pins, swastikas, bondage gear, jackets embroidered 'Belsen was a gas', facial distortion and two fingers at the camera. These bodily messages set out to challenge all that humanitarian society claims to value in favour of that dark side of human history, often left unspoken and better forgotten. These people close to childhood make visible all those things children are said to be ignorant of and adults have learnt to express in carefully licensed ways. Knowledge suppressed in childhood is here written across the bodies of those who declare themselves not-child. In offering themselves up in such a conspicuous way these young people are challenging the camera, daring their presenters to use them for their own ends. They entice the camera, then greet it with a scowl. They force us to ask, with the *Daily Mirror*, 'Who do they think they are?' Any work we do in interpreting the puzzle must take into account that the clues and false trails were first laid by the young people themselves.

Even more disturbing than the challenging content of their self-presentation was its lack of fixity and unpredictability. As fast as they could be catalogued, analysed and defined, so they re-catalogued, reassembled and redefined themselves. The fact that they were *there* became more important than what they said, as young people played games with their definers. The outrageous appearance seduces the camera, but something slips away from behind that spectacular front. They solicit our attention, then refuse its implications. By making themselves visible they make it clear that they cannot be known. The glittering parade of signs, the circus of appearances complete with greasepaint and fancy dress, distracts as it entertains us. This surface has no depth. It is a signifier which belies its signified. It traps the gaze in order to deflect further investigation and forms a cover for the missing identity of an impossible group. This is what Dick Hebdige has described as 'hiding in the light'.

In picturing teenagers there are no secret moments to peep at. The role of the observer is itself called into question. Everything is visible, yet nothing is clear. If young people cannot control the way their image is presented, they can at least make it both challenging and difficult to decipher. As T.R. Fyvel's Teddy Boy informant declared, decked in his eye-catching gear, 'No one can look at the Boys and laugh and get away with it.' These people who are no longer children challenge the controlling gaze.

Yet those who hold the power to make pictures have many strategies with which to win back the right to look. One is to exercise a new form of classification. The issue of age may be reduced in importance in favour of other characteristics which help to make sense of the frightening mix of qualities. Like a strange tribe with its own customs and rituals incomprehensible to a civilised understanding, young people are frequently classified as 'exotic'. Children are destined to become adults, but 'exotic' peoples can be presented as irreducibly different. 'Primitive' tribes are a regular part of colour magazine and travel magazine entertainment, shown as simpler, more emotional, less rational. Their way of life is spectacular and fascinating but may also be amoral, degraded and brutal. To look at the exotic is to look as a tourist, a travel photographer or an anthropologist – to look with the eyes of civilisation at the uncivilised, of the coloniser at the colonised. It is a look which observes in order to control, a vision which is woven into the language of racial subordination. Young people are regularly described as 'tribal' – with all the primitive licence that the word implies. 'The "tribes" of youngsters who dance the night away across Britain all have their own distinctive style – in music, attitudes, dress,' wrote the *Daily Star* in 1980. 'The beat goes on from midnight to breakfast time, inspiring complex and energetic feats of twisting, leaping and high kicks.'

In the *Sunday Times* Ian Jack reported that his friends reacted to his interviews with young people 'as though one had returned from a long stay with the Marsh Arabs'. Constructing their own image with sophisticated irony, young people are put firmly back in their place. Their modern commentary on urban life is translated into a tribal ritual in an urban jungle. Studied self-presentation is rewritten as the least knowing of 'natural' behaviour. Equating young people with the exotic ensures that they retain their childishness, just as 'exotic' peoples themselves are attributed the qualities of childhood. But civilisation's 'other' remains necessary to civilisation's sense of its 'self'. This alien group can express qualities we fear so that they may be intemperately condemned, and qualities we long for so that they may be vicariously enjoyed.

Pushing exoticism to its extreme has been the aim of the professionals of youth. Fashion models, rock musicians, performers who may themselves no longer be young, continue to act out a 'youth' style, recycling ever more spectacular images of rebellion for yet new generations of teenage consumers. In an ironic move, the theme of total rejection could be filtered through that most accepting of all moments, the moment of purchase. The scenario of youth as outsider became one amongst many transformed by the highly conscious image-makers of 1980s style culture. The mid-1980s expansion of youth magazines with zingy and exciting layouts – *Smash Hits, Just 17, No. 1* – expanded the outlets for professionals of youth who became entrepreneurs of style. The new generation of young people eagerly bought the tapes, magazines and posters which bore their image, apparently giving up on the search for a new, uncommodified form of rebellion. The death of the youth cultures came with the perfection of youth consumption.

Not representing youth, but feeding off an image of youth, style magazines like *The Face* and *I–D*, their fragmented visual style echoing youth displacement, have been able to mobilise the themes of nihilism, decadence and a space that appeared to remain in opposition to social norms. 'When the decadence of recent seasons crumbles in disorder (doesn't it always?) there will be no rules and styles – only chaos. You might as well be in bedlam . . . ' was the caption to an advertising feature for 3D (Destroy, Disorientate, Disorder) in *The Face* in September 1985.

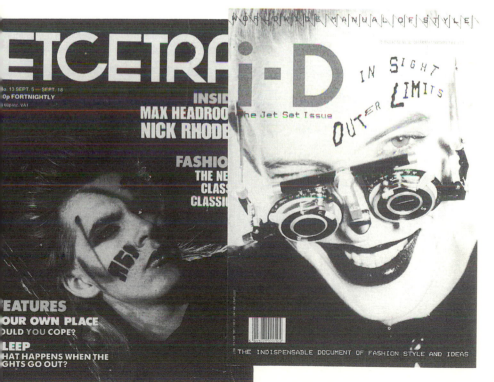

In that confident moment, the art-school style won out and young entrepreneurs, designers and graphic artists enjoyed an unprecedented prosperity. For them life itself became a media event, and the everyday world was portrayed as a playground for those without ties or commitments. As it had from its ambiguous beginnings, the spectacle of youth continued to intertwine marketing needs with young people's own dramatic acts of personal rejection, and the social displacement of a group whose uncertain position was not so easily dispelled.

Another strategy for dealing with the impertinence of youth has been to produce an imagery which seeks to degrade its subjects. By the late 1970s the use of drugs, which had given rise to the psychedelic dream of the 1960s, had become a sign of youth excess that could lead only to disaster. The impossible position young people are expected to take could result in early death – the theme of 'No future' at its most literal. The threat of destruction posed by the image of young people included that of their own self-destruction. Sid Vicious was only one in a series of youthful performers to act out this scenario in public. In a desperate move of recuperation even he was shown in a family context, accompanied by his mother. 'I want to self-destruct myself,' he said. 'Look at my arms. That's a bottle scar from when I cut myself. Look at my chest . . . ' In an interview two

FREEDOM: Vicious with his mother after his release on bail — just one day before he died.

years before he died in 1979, he repeated, 'I'll probably die before I'm 25. But I'll have lived the way I wanted to.' His death continued to be evoked by his followers. 'Charlie reckons he will be dead by his 21st birthday,' reported the *Daily Mirror* in 1980, 'and he's happy to know he'll die a skinhead. "I want to die like Sid," he says.'

Self-destruction and the decaying body of the drug-taker confirmed the despair which lay behind the claim to ecstatic pleasure. The huddled bodies and downcast eyes of the *Daily Mirror*'s 'shock report' of December 1985 are echoed in the Health Education Council's advertisement 'Heroin screws you up'. By contrast with its jaunty 1983 feature 'Bloody kids', the *Mirror*'s 'Junk generation' of

THESE 2.30am YESTERDAY. KIDS ARE ON THE RUN

JUNK

Ellen, Ian, Debbie, Eric, Runaways. Meet them on Page 2

GENERATION

THE Mirror

FORWARD WITH BRITAIN

THIS 2.30am YESTERDAY GIRL IS ON HEROIN

1985 presented a typology of despair. Now we are introduced to the dosser, the runaway, the racist, the hooligan, the thug, the rapist. This imagery sternly refuses any playful collaboration with its subjects. It seeks to portray 'the depths of hell'. The language which accompanies the pictures is a bitter language of total rejection: 'Joey Lamb is trash. A junk kid littering a junk world.' These young people 'are difficult to sympathise with and impossible to understand'.

Is this the best future we can offer our school leavers?

There are now more young people out of work than at any time since the war.

In some areas that's 1 in 3. And they're not work-shy hooligans, they're victims of the economic facts of life.

They've applied for jobs – in some cases they've applied for dozens – and they've been told that without a skill or work experience they haven't a chance.

Which makes them teenage rejects. Turned down without trial.

Youth Opportunities Programme.

The Youth Opportunities Programme is a new plan to help employers help young people, even if they can't offer any permanent jobs.

It's based on the best elements of existing schemes that have succeeded in helping as many as 8 out of 10 participants into jobs.

The idea is extremely simple: If you can take in young people for up to six months, introducing them to the benefits and disciplines of work, we will pay them £19.50 a week. And there are no National Insurance contributions or tax returns to worry about.

They get invaluable experience, training and the chance to earn a reference that proves their worth. You get a chance to give them a future without having to take anyone on permanently – unless you want to.

The alternative.

The only alternative is a growing number of young people who feel discarded by 'the system' and a smaller pool of trained and enthusiastic people for industry to draw upon.

And, if nothing's done, the inescapable truth is that by the end of this year the situation will be even worse.

Which is why the Programme is backed by the government, the CBI and the TUC.

How it works.

We have offices all over the country and our staff are eager to give employers every detail of the scheme. At the same time, these offices keep in close touch with all the bodies concerned with unemployed young people in your area.

Which makes them uniquely qualified to help you help young people.

If you're interested in participating in the Programme, our staff will help you plan an introduction to work for young people that will benefit them without disturbing the normal running of your business.

You are then free to choose the young men and women you feel have the most to offer – and whose future will be brighter as a result of training and experience under your guidance.

Then it's up to the Youth Opportunities Programme to make sure that your involvement is as trouble-free and rewarding as possible. Give a young person a chance, and we will do the rest.

What to do.

Get the full story from Roger Panton, Manpower Services Commission, Department G5, Selkirk House, 166 High Holborn, London WC1V 6PF. Tel. 01-836 1213.

Our future workforce depends on it.

YOUTH OPPORTUNITIES PROGRAMME MSC

The language of the *Daily Mirror* was not always so extreme. In previous years it had produced issues which, in a mood of humanist realism, presented a sympathetic view of youth unemployment, recognising that many youngsters simply dropped out between the cracks of society rather than placing themselves outside in a deliberate act of refusal. But the idea of degradation has a more powerful pull. At the end of the 1970s advertisements showing young people thrown aside like so much garbage were used to promote youth training schemes. By the end of the 1980s the image had been overtaken by reality. Newspapers now reported young people begging in railway stations, sleeping in cardboard boxes and sheltering in shop doorways as the problem of homelessness was added to that of unemployment. They were on the streets, not asserting their right to use those spaces but because there was nowhere else for them to go.

THE EXPRESS LOOKS AT THE PLIGHT OF THE THOUSANDS OF HOMELESS

Day-to-day living in the hell-hole . . . Sarah "at home" in the Bullring, Waterloo, sums up the loneliness of the long-distance slummer better than words can say

Twilight world of the cardboard kids

By NEIL MACKWOOD

‘It is a frequent story of rebellion and failure’

NEXT week Ian McKay and his 17 year old fiancee Jasmine will make themselves look as smart as possible and gather with their friends to get married at the Church of St. John with St. Andrew, Waterloo, just like any other loving young couple.

There is nothing unusual in these circumstances except that the future Mr and Mrs McKay will have to haul themselves out of a wooden crate in a sort of underground cavern called The ‘home.

The euphemistically is a vast hole on the loo Bridge around six directions. It from view from all ture into its howe the walkways.

At night the *ative. It is he* *people and it* *alfresco diss*

Jasmine educated a growing up young p selves o society

The to ad mate has The figur

the streets of the capital, but charities like Shelter reckon around 56,000 16- to 19-year-olds experience homelessness each year.

What is com sations is th ing youn tion. yo

spending in an amusement arcade the 15 his father gave him.

He spent four days sleeping rough. After being picked up by the police he was sent to a hostel and now is settle ‘omfortable one-bedroom fla ng r

came to London to see a skinhead band called Screwdriver and then didn't have the money for the fare home. So she is stuck in a stinking underground hell-hole unable to find a roof over her head with no prospects in sight of being reunited with her baby.

Jasmine, the bride-to-be, ran away from a children's home and now shares her box in the Bullring with Ian, 30, who is frequently drunk, and their two They say they need £3

Taking comfort . . . Jasmine, 17, with her puppy, Whisky

113

In the public narratives of the last twenty years there has been another danger associated with young people who are disaffected or rebellious: they could become part of a politics of opposition. In the slippery movement of definitions of youth there has been an easy shift from existential rejection to social rejection, from alternative cultures to oppositional politics. The student movement of the 1960s and the school student demonstrations of the 1970s were much deplored in the newspaper dramas of politicised youth. One of the strategies for dealing with the challenge they posed was the constant reassurance that since these people are really children, they are not to be taken seriously; another was to circulate pictures of nice, fresh-faced youngsters who have no reason to rebel and can act as exemplars for youth. They express a politics of conformity, even of conservatism.

Perhaps the most effective strategy for bringing the image of youth under control has been the search for 'nice kids'. This means ripping away the mask to reveal what lies behind it and bring the 'real' teenager under public scrutiny. 'Are they really as horrible as they appear?' asked the *News of the World*, and gave the answer 'No': 'Underneath those mad mohican hairdos, startling make-up and way-out clothes are typical teenagers.' When a quieter, more 'real-istic' photographic mode forces the image of young people back into the mundane world of trivial concerns, a much more reassuring view of youth emerges.

Such pictures stress the ordinariness of the young people they show. Unadorned by make-up or fancy dress, their faces undistorted by scowls, they accept the gaze of the camera in a relaxed, if slightly tentative way. The gesture of removing the mask reveals above all their childishness. It shows them to be weak and insecure. Their challenge is defused.

The smiling faces and neatly clad bodies of nice kids are frequently found in the local press, which speaks directly to friends and relatives and whose narratives are less likely to assume the moral and metaphorical rhetoric of the national press. Here we find young people who have won competitions, gained high exam marks and proved their excellence in a variety of fields from classical music to sport. Their clothing is casual, or they wear school uniform or sports gear; their hair is tidy, their expressions are relaxed or smiling. This is what we would hope to find behind the mask of youth – adolescents, maturing discreetly, learning to put childhood behind them but not ashamed to retain an appropriate degree of childish-ness. These young people will open bank accounts, go to universities and not get caught up in student politics unless, like young Tory William Hague, they can 'speak with the voice of youth with an edge of maturity'.

Jubilee gold for tots

's are
ugust
rwich

more to
Football
nbledon's
played in
n can get

h Lane.
's price,
is £22,
P's and
e vice-
k Band

at Har-
of Clive

aders Leices-
while Surrey
norgan.

personal
in the
Sunday
er Mills
ter two

wnley 5
e of 25.03
ohn Hall
d fifth in

Motors
day in

aurie
in the
pthall
as 25
(Cam-

atch at
perfor-
comp-

Every
32 Boro
teams in
Youth Gar
Borough
differs
youth

The
Game
Cryst
Sports
6/7.

● Full of confidence, members of the contigent from All Saints primary school, Fulham High Street relax before competing in the Hammersmith Schools' Jubilee Sports.
Photo: Kemp.

Nearly 800 youngsters from 25 schools competed in Hammersmith Primary Schools' Jubilee Sports watched by a record 700 spectators at and Under: M. Fisher, Miles Coverdale, P. Pierre, Addison, F Semple, Sher- Girls Relay Over 10: Kenmont, Ellerslie, Miles Coverdale

THE BOY WHO TOOK THE TORY CONFERENCE BY STORM

Just William...

BLACKPOOL belonged to William Hague yesterday. He's 16.

His speech to the Tory Party conference—and to the nation on TV—brought Mrs Thatcher, Jim Prior and Sir Keith Joseph to their feet like benign aunt and uncles.

Here was the voice of youth with an edge of maturity putting everybody, Tory and Labour alike, in their place.

All Governments, including Mrs Thatcher's, he said, 'must get out of the people's way'.

In 30 years, many of the people in the Winter Gardens wouldn't be in a position to care anyway—but I will be, and I want to be free'.

To round off a day of triumph, he even appeared in a television discussion with Sir Geoffrey Howe, the Shadow Chancellor.

William's political ambitions began in 1974 when he abandoned his all-consuming hobby of war games for the role of potential MP.

His bedroom wall in the large house near Rotherham where he lives with his parents and three sisters is decorated with an election poster of Mrs Thatcher and the names of every MP.

Memory

His photographic memory supplies all the election facts and figures on each of them.

The family runs a small but successful mineral water business.

His mother, Mrs Stella Hague, was too busy washing

William with Mrs Thatcher : 'Government must get out of people's way.'

liam wants to change. He would have the same views if he lived in a council house.

'He has thought it all out for himself without any prompt-

He has nine 'O' levels and hopes to go to Oxford and become an MP, even Prime Minister.

Meanwhile, he reads Han- d every night and spends

His headmaster, Mr John Brothwell, said: 'I'm delighted for him—and that he showed we at a comprehensive are not suppressing talent.'

115

Nice kids often appear in uniform. It may be school uniform, a chorister's outfit or the uniform of a body like the Boy Scouts, still organising youngsters eighty-odd years after its foundation. Here the exotica of young people's clothing is set aside in favour of a reminder of the past. Since the 1890s the youth club movement has made an effort to get urban children off the streets. Organisations like the Boys' Brigade, the Band of Hope, the Girl Guides, aimed to tame the unruly youth of the working class and take them away from the temptations of the urban jungle into the fresh air of the countryside. Streetwise inner-city kids were taught the forest-wise ways of North American Indians.

Uniform adds a sense of discipline and respectability to the image of young people. But the picture of young soldiers or cadets in military uniform is more difficult. Amidst a chorus of condemnation of youth violence, this image makes violence legitimate. The 1989 United Nations Convention on the Rights of the Child forbids its signatories to enrol children in the armed forces under the age of sixteen – although many of its other provisions take eighteen as the age below which children must be protected. In Britain some cadets have entered the forces as young as fifteen and a half. But in the image, the uniform itself suggests a structured hierarchy that will keep the young people within its ranks firmly controlled.

Out on the streets, however, the 'vicious generation' – the *Sun*'s description – has rejected any form of control: 'Terror is a modern fact of life. Increasingly Britain is a nation that walks in fear of its young.' Adolescent anomie, the problem of unemployment, youth entertainment and the delights of the youth parade – all these must be seen against a background of periodic and increasingly apocalyptic reports of youth disorder. This is where young people leave the features pages and burst on to the front pages as news. Fears that have been hinted at, dramatised or parodied become brute facts, and 'youth', which symbolises all that is chaotic and irrational, seems to throw off all constraint and act out its dreadful potential. 'Their delight in injury and destruction was appalling,' reported the *Sunday Mirror* of the Brixton riots in 1981. 'Much as you understand the tremendous pressures they are under, the sight and sound of children of 14 and 16 crowing and bragging about inflicting pain brings you to the depths of despair . . . A society that produces such callousness among its young has many disturbing questions to ask itself.'

Daily Mail

WEDNESDAY, JULY 8, 1981   12p

BOTHAM QUITS AS CAPTAIN —BACK PAGE

New rioting breaks out in London

HUNDREDS of black youths went on the rampage in north London last night, smashing shop windows and attacking police.

Some 500 extra police were drafted into Wood Green after a man had his throat cut and another was stabbed during the clashes between youths and police.

The Special Patrol Group was called in when about 400 black youngsters began looting shops in Wood Green High Road and Turnpike Lane.

Several times police with riot shields

charged threatening gangs who broke windows to loot a men's outfitters, a jewellers and an off-licence.

The rioters started fires in wastebins up and down Wood Green High Road where a multi-million pound shopping precinct was recently opened.

Police with shields attempted to drive them from the High Road. They were backed by dozens of youngsters then ran off down near-by Green Lanes.

Police cars were pelted with bricks, dustbins and beer cans.

The looting was being carried out by youths who smashed through shop

fronts. One used a tailor's dummy as a weapon before a second rank moved in to help themselves to the property.

A sergeant with the SPG said that he saw youths looting a shop. 'They ran off, and I found one lad with a gaping wound in his chest which I staunched with a tee-shirt from the looted window.'

The SPG man said that youths were smashing windows 'as if they were goading the police.'

Three cars were overturned and attempts were made to set them on fire, but police dispersed the youths.

Local people said that outsiders

from Tottenham and Walthamstow had come into the area to provoke trouble, but the youths involved claimed they were responding to harsh police treatment.

Trouble started at about 9 p.m., as small groups gathered near Turnpike Lane Tube station.

Police, who were expecting it because of incidents the day before when there was a break-in at a Woolworth store, were there in large numbers, moving the youths on.

At midnight police said 93 had been arrested.

And after the problem children looting in Liverpool the question is—

DON'T THEIR PARENTS CARE?

Criminal greed and Yobbism rampant . . . looters pillaging a Liverpool supermarket   Picture: BARRY FARRELL

AT MIDNIGHT, by the red light of the fires they have lit, the young of Liverpool look truly scary, like stunted demons emerging from the shadows with throwing arms raised.

At mid-morning, filing into juvenile

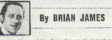

By BRIAN JAMES

these past three nights from the one they hold on the back benches of Parliament or on party platforms.

London's Hatton Garden is a diamond market. Liverpool's is a street of drab grey buildings, of which the juvenile court is the cleanest.

But only on the outside.

As you file up the stairs, you see at once that

Thus the first of the night's crop of 'rioters' appears. Boy, 12, charged with looting cigarettes from a shop at 1.30 a.m. Everyone is very careful not to make him feel overawed or awkward. 'Stand here, John. Is your mother here? Oh good. Now you just listen carefully to what is said.'

What is said, by the police solicitor, is that Liverpool faces 'a situation without precedent' that below stairs all is chaos. He can ask only for remands in this and every case to come. And that bail, please, should be allowed only under rigid conditions—such as a curfew from 6 p.m. to 8 a.m.

Instantly the boy's rigid conditions, on her feet. He has to carry a flag in an Orange Day parade on Saturday, and she has already paid £200 for his get-up. Couldn't he stay out later than we might? 'As he couldn't,' says the magistrate and boy and mother go sadly away.

117

From the Teddy Boy gang fights of the 1950s to the anti-poll tax riots of 1990, these most dramatic of public narratives put the image of unruly youth at their centre. Arising in different political contexts and involving different social groups, these events – from the fighting between Black people and police at successive Notting Hill carnivals to the periodic recurrence of football hooliganism – nevertheless fill a similar position in the structured dramas of the popular press. Central to these dramas is the image of the crowd – young people gathered together in an undifferentiated, unstructured group, moving in unpredictable directions, running all over the place, carried along by a euphoria which allows the release of what is here described as 'violence'. The main concern in the reporting of these different events has been to identify and describe this moment of violence, and to characterise its perpetrators. Although later pulled back and knitted into the continuing flow of the narrative, these hectic moments seem to stand for something beyond, expressing a universal nightmare. 'Violence' is seen as a unitary, irreducible phenomenon which cannot be explained or analysed – indeed, any attempt to explain it is rejected as an attempt to excuse it. Feverish reporting casts young people of all sorts as objects of intemperate abuse and mortal fear. They are 'undisciplined, prejudiced and arrogant hooligans, dead set on overturning order, reason and free speech'. They are wreckers, young thugs, animals, beasts and a threat to our sanity. They are 'stunted demons, emerging from the shadows with throwing arms raised'. The language pushes against the limits of humanity itself, provoking without examining questions about the division between humans and beasts and about forms of human behaviour which border on the margins of tolerance.

The language of the tribal, the primitive and the savage gained a new significance as Black youth took a prominent part in the urban riots of the 1980s. 'St Paul's, revolt of the lost tribe' was how the *Observer* headlined the Bristol disturbances of 1980. 'England' was regularly invoked as the epitome of civilisation, the antithesis of uncontrol. 'This is not England. It's just madness', a policeman told the *Daily Express* after the Broadwater Farm riot in 1985. Blackness, primitiveness and a lust for violence were ideas which came together in an easy slide from metaphor to description. 'Many experts predict that life will only change for Britain's Blacks by bloodshed,' wrote Jean Richie in the *Sun*. 'Amazingly, some would even welcome it.'

Photographs search for the moment of action, the dynamism of movement, the 'throwing arm raised', waiting for the rioter to clutch the petrol bomb or the looter to smash the window. Pictures are occasionally cropped, or the figure may be outlined if the action is sufficiently dramatic, but most often the edges of the frame are pushed back to include as many actions as possible. In one notable

1981

> The next riots will take place in Birmingham and Manchester 9

—Jeff Crawford, community relations officer

DAILY Mirror
Monday, April 13, 1981   12p

Battle of Brixton

THE SHAPE OF THINGS TO COME

THE BLOODY scenes of violence and destruction which scarred Brixton at the weekend will be repeated over and over again, it was claimed yesterday.

Black community leaders meeting to discuss the riots warned that "police intolerance" will visit new outbreaks even in other parts of the country.

"The next riots will take place in Birmingham and Manchester's Moss Side" said Haringey Community Relations Officer Jeff Crawford.

By ROGER TODD

THE BATTLE RAGES: Youths, white and black, hurl their barrage of missiles at point blank range as police attempt to take cover behind riot shields

PLEASE TURN TO PAGES 2, 3, 6, 7 and Centre Pages

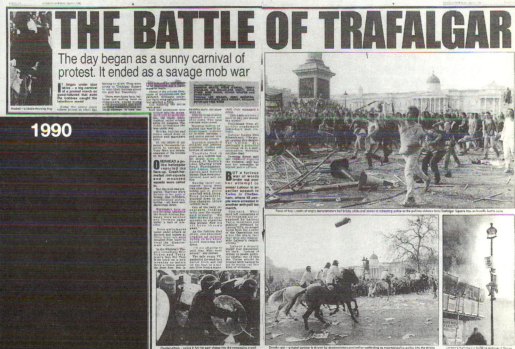

THE BATTLE OF TRAFALGAR

The day began as a sunny carnival of protest. It ended as a savage mob war

1990

Forces of fury — mobs of angry demonstrators hurl bricks, sticks and stones at retreating police as the poll tax violence turns Trafalgar Square into a horrific battle zone

example a high-angle picture of a Brixton street, with police behind their riot shields at one end and youths 'with throwing arms raised' at the other, spread across the front and back pages of the *Daily Mirror*. Fire, dust and mêlée played an important role in the imagery of the riots, amongst a landscape of broken windows and burning buildings and vehicles.

This is the most extreme of images of escape – but the pleasurable chaos is rapidly taken hold of and pulled back into the flow of the narrative as the theme becomes the familiar one of control. The aim is twofold: to reassert authority within the frame, and to use the news photographs themselves as evidence of crimes committed. 'If you know 'em, SHOP 'EM' headlined *The People* after the poll tax demo of March 1990 above mug shots of rioters enlarged from news pictures. Photographers and readers are separated from any empathy with the demonstrators and drawn into the drama. They become collaborators in reasserting public order and adult values.

Within the frame, order is restored as the mobile crowd is visually

1972   1981

fragmented and the police move in to make arrests. When escape attempts take extreme forms, repression may legitimately be violent. One of the most familiar images that accompany narratives of trouble on the streets is that of a young person, often black, struggling in the arms of several police officers. It is an image which visually detaches a single individual from the crowd and demonstrates their subjection to punishment. Youth is finally put in its place: 'A few moments before he was confident and aggressive. Now they drag him away screaming for Mummy.'

1981   1990

6

Sex and sexuality

Doubling the image

> The difficulty, the contradictory struggle, comes exactly in respect
> of identity, of the maintenance of sexual identity.
>
> Stephen Heath, *The Sexual Fix*

So much hinges on the categorisation of male and female that
distinctions built into the language make it a condition of humanity
itself. It is only when we are told whether a newborn is a boy or a girl
that we can allow the child to enter the world of human society and
refer to 'it' with one, and only one, of those mutually exclusive,
domineering, erotic and culturally explosive terms 'him' or 'her'. It is
only in relation to these two opposing categories that our behaviour
can be socially appropriate. We live in a sexed society. Yet things are
never quite as clear cut as they seem. The difference is by no means
taken for granted. In itself it becomes the focus of playfulness and
excess in the available imagery, a source of endless exploration and
experimentation. As it seeks to produce two alternative types of
individual, it states, restates and overstates differences that at one
moment seem oh so natural, oh so obvious, and at the next so fragile
that they must be strictly enforced.

'Babies come into the world predisposed to behave in typically
masculine and feminine ways. Non-sexist parents can wipe out all
our toy stores, television shows and picture books to no avail. As far
as we can tell, girls become girls and boys become boys without
them', wrote Sara Stein in a study of non-sexist child-rearing in 1983.

Five years later, a presentation in *Woman* headed 'Would you buy your son a doll?' echoed the point: 'Even at play, today's children are practising skills they'd have needed 10,000 years ago', wrote child psychologist Dr John Richer. They were rehearsing a theme that had become increasingly familiar during the 1980s – sometimes stated triumphantly, sometimes regretfully: feminism has made its point and is no longer needed. Western society is to be congratulated on modernising gender relations and painlessly adjusting their grosser inequalities. We can now settle back into a world where the brute facts of gender will continue to impress us with their old, immutable forms. No amount of tinkering with cultural patterns can affect those inbuilt relations of power and desire. 'Men don't want their sons to be effeminate, so they go for masculine toys', Gerry Masters of the National Association of Toy Retailers told *Woman*. As sexual difference is explored with relish across the range of public imagery, our attention is drawn again and again to the effort that goes into maintaining it as a fact. Even the image of babies may be doubled, emphasising that childhood is made up of two types rather than one. When a contrast is needed, male babies tend to be shown as active, assertive and upright, female babies as passive and relaxed. Strategies of differentiation change. What remains constant is the assertion of difference itself.

The visual conventions for indicating the sex of children range from the minimal, in which a line drawing eliminates all but the essentials, to the maximal, drawing on all the resources of advertising photography. Either way, our recognition of the children in the pictures we encounter is instant, involuntary and unquestioned. A line drawing, like the one by the inimitable children's illustrator Dick Bruna, used on the front page of the *Observer* magazine, may extract every possible detail to leave only the simplest indicators of difference. The difference centres on the presentation of the girl. She is recognised by the use of curves rather than straight lines and angles, and by an *addition*. She has six extra lines to stand for hairs.

She is what is described in linguistics as the marked term. Femininity deviates from the norm of the male. But as we look at the picture,
we are the ones who bring to it our understanding that femininity is
softer and more decorative. *Our* reading of the image is laden with
the potency of that commonplace distinction, and it is the work *we*
do that completes its meanings. As we look we are forced to bring
into play a series of judgements and understandings across a whole
range of social and emotional fields. This network includes social
roles, the living arrangements of households, child-rearing, power
relations between the sexes, sexual attraction, erotic relations and our
very sense of ourselves. All that hinges on a few little hairs. A
distinction between 'sex', which is biologically given, and 'gender',
which is social and constructed, although analytically useful, is not
by itself enough to deal with the interplay of the different parts of
this system – in particular the way in which the whole complex of
social arrangements is underpinned by the forces of sexuality and
desire that confirm us in our personal identity. A single picture, by
enforcing an act of differentiation, refers us to those systems of
social, biological and psychical arrangements and secures our place
within them. It is only when we pause to consider this process more
closely that its instability becomes suddenly, startlingly visible.

It is in the imagery of advertising that the details of differentiation
between the sexes is explored most fully. Advertisements celebrate
present pleasures and open themselves to challenging and critical
meanings at their peril. So it comes about that as we look at the
construction of consumer roles we are also looking at the construction of gender roles. Sexual difference is confirmed in the moments of
purchase and consumption. The commercial imperative insists that
no detail should be out of place to trouble the affirmative impression
of an advertisement, yet the overstatement may itself be so great that
the security of the message is shaken. There is an impression that
everything must be held firmly in place to ward off the possibility of
the escape of meanings and secure these precisely directed messages.

A pair of advertisements for Heinz tinned foods appeared in the
late 1970s, at the height of feminist campaigns about the representation of women and girls. They set out to persuade mothers to buy
food for their children that is nourishing, convenient and, like the
children's chosen activities, enjoyable. As we, too, take pleasure in
these delightful pictures, once more we find ourselves confirming –
and indeed enjoying – the radical differences they pose between
male and female, boys and girls. The photographs employ a casual
naturalism. It seems as if we are catching the children unawares, as is
the adult's right. Yet these are no documentary pictures, snapping
the world as it passes before the lens. They have been expensively set
up, carefully lit and framed, every detail controlled in what Erving

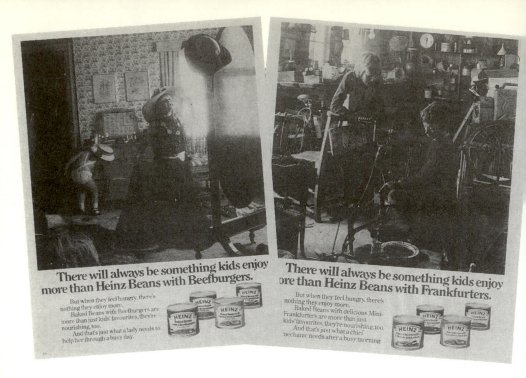

There will always be something kids enjoy more than Heinz Beans with Beefburgers.

But when they feel hungry, there's nothing they enjoy more. Baked Beans with Beefburgers are more than just kids' favourites, they're nourishing, too. And that's just what a lady needs to help her through a busy day.

There will always be something kids enjoy ore than Heinz Beans with Frankfurters.

But when they feel hungry, there's nothing they enjoy more. Baked Beans with delicious Mini-Frankfurters are more than just kids' favourites, they're nourishing, too. And that's just what a chief mechanic needs after a busy morning.

Goffman called 'commercial syncretism'. They construct a heightened realism, bathed in the golden glow of a possible happiness. Both pictures are organised around gender. Both are crammed full of details. But no detail is innocent; each is the consequence of the presence of a male or female person, creating a harmonious totality. Nothing must confuse our expectations nor hamper our task of discriminating between the two. The props create a space that in the one case can be filled only by a boy, and in the other only by a girl. The activities and positioning of the bodies follow patterns we recognise as characteristically male or female. The girl with her head bent back displays her body; the boys are bent forward over a purposeful task. The girls are in a bedroom, playing at being adult women. The boys are in a garden shed full of tools, oil cans, paintbrushes and the paraphernalia of masculine tasks. Unlike the girls they are not pretending but engaged in authentic work, mending a bike. In the series of antitheses set up between the pictures the controlling opposition between male and female brings into play the associated oppositions between indoors and outdoors, clean and dirty, play and work, self-absorption and object-absorption.

Once more, in reading the image, it is we who contribute to the completeness of its meanings. In an active process of continuous differentiation we reallocate each other to its place – bikes to boys, dressing-up clothes to girls – and repress any slippage between the two. Confident in its own aggressive statement of difference, the imagery assumes a reading by people who are themselves secure in their own sex/gender positioning. That assumption helps to establish a sense of social maleness or femaleness despite any insecurity in living out those categories. Homosexuality, lesbianism, any form of sexual nonconformity, seems inconceivable in their comfortably divided world. Pictures like these calm our anxieties, helping us to be aware, as Stephen Heath put it in *The Sexual Fix*, 'of the absolute fact of difference, yet needing to deal with the simultaneous absence of difference in any one individual'.

Throughout the 1980s and into the 1990s public imagery has continued to reiterate the need to differentiate. Lovable, grubby young boys, each with a bold and impudent grin, are placed beside coy young girls, their soulful expressions already posing the enigma of sexual knowledge. The boys aspire to adulthood, but the girls seduce. For children in these pre-teenage years, gender and sexuality are confirmed not by their relations with each other but by their contrast with each other and their differing relations with adults.

Advertisements use children as a justification for adult behaviour and patterns of consumption, offering models of good parenting. They also show children as trainees, learning to take their place as appropriately gendered adults. The girl's training for domestic labour, child-rearing and the sexual gratification of men figures in many an advertisement for washing machines, toys and toiletries. Mothers are helped by daughters around the house, and initiate them into the use of clothes and cosmetics. The boy's training for physical labour, intellectual control and leisure choices dominates

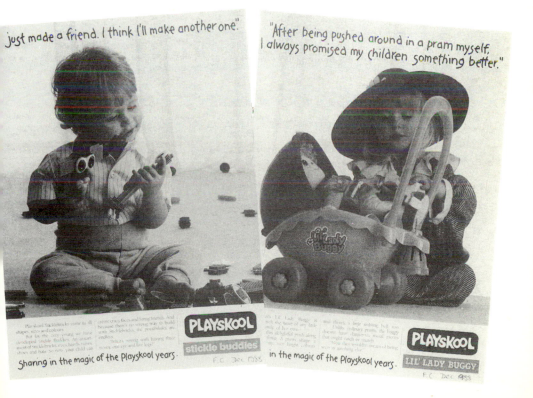

"just made a friend. I think I'll make another one."

"After being pushed around in a pram myself, I always promised my children something better."

Sharing in the magic of the Playskool years.

in the magic of the Playskool years.

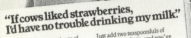

"If cows liked strawberries, I'd have no trouble drinking my milk."

Kids need the goodness of milk. But sometimes it's difficult getting them to drink milk on its own.

Luckily you can solve that problem instantly and also give them extra vitamins.

Just add two teaspoonfuls of **Nesquik**, and stir, and you've got a delicious strawberry, chocolate, raspberry or banana flavour drink they'll enjoy till the cows come home.

In four delicious tasting flavours with added vitamins A, B, and C.

'Nesquik' makes a good thing even better.

Nestlé **Nesquik** STRAWBERRY FLAVOUR

...aspberry **Nesquik** is right ...arget"

...need the goodness of ...t sometimes it's ...etting them to drink ...s own.

...you can solve that ...stantly and also ...xtra vitamins.

Just add two teaspoonfuls of **Nesquik**, and stir, and you've got a delicious raspberry flavour drink that's a winner every time.

In raspberry, strawberry, chocolate or banana flavour with added vitamins A, B, and C.

...makes a good thing even better.

Nestlé **Nesquik** RASPBERRY FLAVOUR

59

---

woman AND Savlon

KIDS TODAY here's what the...

At last—the results of our nationwide survey on how our children view the world we live in. As always you'll be amazed, amused and sometimes alarmed by what they have to say. Jemima Harrison reports. Picture by Paul Dunn

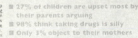

When *WOMAN* teamed up with Savlon—the leading name in first aid—to run a special survey to find out how children felt about their lives, we ...helmed by the response. ...nions, feelings, joys ...how are those of the ...n who filled in

...stance. ...at only ...ple ...hat ...

- 27% of children are upset most by their parents arguing
- 98% think taking drugs is silly
- Only 3% object to their mothers going out to work
- 31% of youngsters are frightened by the thought of nuclear war
- 26% of children say Neighbours is their favourite TV programme
- Nine out of ten 13-year-olds have suffered serious injury, illness, bereavement, assault or parental separation

OUR POCKET MONEY

...majority of children (62 per cent) say ...happy with the amount of pocket ...y get. The average is £1.76, with ...and under netting 76p a week ...s £3.65. Six and seven-year-...kely to blow the lot straight ...toys and comics (29 per ...ent of kids save theirs for ...13 per cent of 11-year-olds ...y for something special.

OUR WORLD

Children are concerned about war (27 per cent), crime (23 per cent), poverty (20 per cent), AIDS (14 per cent), smoking (nine per cent) and unemployment (two per cent). They saw taking drugs (98 per cent), stealing money (96 per cent), playing with fireworks (96 per cent), cross-ing a busy road (96 per cent), throwing knives (95 per cent), smoking (92 per cent), and drinking alcohol (70 per cent) as being very silly indeed.

Ninety-one per cent of six-...-olds like their teachers, ...only 41 per cent of 14-...olds. And while 85 to 88 ...ent of six to 10-year-olds ...the police, only 62 per ...f 14-year-olds do. Fifty ...r cent believe they'll ...aven when they die.

WE KNO...

Children certainly kno... for them. Over 80 ... that chocolate, c... drinks are bad (a... eat them!), and ... vegetables and s... Only 68 per cent... hamburgers might b...

Girls seem more a... of which foods to... older kids are, the ... are to choose a ...

As to what ... what's not, t... said they wou... distinguish ... ucts, while ... dren would ... expect dan... to be kept...

It's clea... and colour... ant. White... blue are c... "safest" colou... 55 and 64 p... black the mai... for 57 per cent... Warning pro... coffin or a skull is... scary by 57 percen... the inflammable ... symbols at 46 an... A cross was se... by 41 percent... per cent. M... pensive note...

There's jo...

WE...

Funny noises i... per cent (45 ... olds). Forty-o... year-olds ima... the bed...

Nearly half ... "rarely" and ... "never". If t... the night, 3... sleep, and 3... to their pare...

Asked wh... frightened ... most. F... Kruger, ... 18-rated ... m a r e ... Street, w... tioned by ... cent of 14... per cent of... Being mu... scares 47 p... Being attacke... second at 14 p... getting lost at ... Strangers fo... people children ...

...films ...news ...ular

128

advertisements for sports equipment, TVs, insurance and other 'masculine' fields. The division has remained remarkably consistent, despite the arrival of free-flowing independent childhood and the 'new man' about the house. It is predominantly mothers who serve their sons with food, medicine and other forms of care. Sons already adopt a masculine role towards their mothers, accepting and indeed demanding their services, and even claiming the right to discipline the adult woman through critical looks and commentary on bodily appearance.

In the Heinz advertisements the boys' world is shown as self-sufficient. By contrast, the picture of the girls is centred on a mirror. The older girl is preparing herself to be looked at by another. Her position just off-centre of the frame causes her to display her decorated body to the viewer, just as, within the picture, she is displaying it to herself. The mirror confirms her image of herself for another, created as another would want to see it. Luce Irigaray argues that woman creates for herself a mask in the image required of her by man, adjusting to what she takes to be a male view of womanhood. The mirror is thus a central icon of what it means to be a woman, and the little girl in the advertisement is already rehearsing her role. But the mirror suggests more than a future relationship for the little girl. It creates a present link between the child in the picture and the grown men who may look at it. The target audience for this advertisement is the purchasing mother, but whenever a little girl appears in the frame there is always an implied audience of adult men to whom such an image carries a potentially sexual meaning.

The imagery of gender differentiation has proved infinitely flexible. Over the last twenty years it has had its progressive moments, only to find the old distinctions reasserting themselves in newer forms. The younger the child, the easier it is to show both sexes playing with building bricks or Lego. But the world of toys remains strictly divided. Boys have Action Man, girls have Barbie dolls. Boys do not have tea sets, dolls' houses, Care Bears or My Little Pony. Girls do not have weapons of war, micromachines or radio-controlled cars. Non-sexist parents faced with this chasm are caught up in acts of discrimination eagerly embraced by the children themselves. 'Lots of manufacturers advertise and package their toys for both girls and boys. But research tells them that sometimes it can be a waste of time and money. Girls simply don't buy the toy and manufacturers also risk alienating boys by linking them with girls at all', wrote toy retailer Gerry Masters.

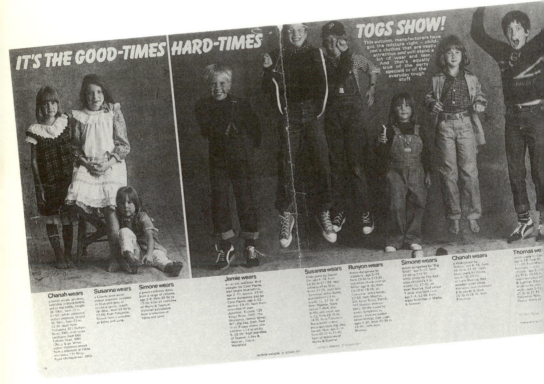

A modernisation of attitudes is constantly pulled back to the statement of difference that is ensured by the marking of girls as inferior. Boys just don't want to be linked with them. So, girls and boys can be shown wearing jeans, tracksuits and T-shirts for energetic activities, but girls must also have skirts and frilly dresses for special occasions. Girls may learn welding along with the rest of the class, but their shoes must have a more decorative shape. Times may change, but the feminine remains the market term in a difference that always subordinates. For the indicators of difference, like those extra hairs in the Dick Bruna drawing, are on the feminine body. That body must display the effort that has been made to ensure it is pleasing to look at. Here social differentiation is returned to a biological difference that is always underpinned by erotic sexuality. For in this rigorously heterosexual regime, the drab differentiation based on housework, childcare, unequal pay and all the other innumerable moments is finally secured by the thrilling potential of sexual excitement.

Times are changing and so are we.
K Shoes.

The baby is a vamp

There is a fantasy for girls that resonates through the imagery of childhood. It appears in girls' books and comics and is filtered through the imagery of young girls in advertisements and magazine features. It is the fantasy of the princess who becomes a bride. In the storybooks she wears a long dress, often white, which makes it difficult to do anything more than romp gently in the palace grounds. Long golden hair and a fair skin are axiomatic – this princess is almost never Black. She usually wears a crown. Servants and admirers pay homage to her status and her beauty and take good care of her. Her every need is catered for. Dressing up, being treated as someone special, being beautiful – these themes launch young girls into the adult world, even in the sophisticated 1990s. In contests like Miss Pears and Miss Mini UK, the prettiest little girl is crowned princess. Her specialness prefigures the moment when she colludes

in her own subordination and becomes a bride, surrounded in her turn by little princesses/bridesmaids. This hoped-for moment is anticipated by the swirling graphics of those comic books where every girl is a romantic heroine. It is also prefigured by all those flowing-haired, seductive young women who look out of the pages of contemporary magazines, to be mirrored in the imagined gaze of the viewing man. The imagery of young girls hints at that point, so exciting to adult men, when she makes the transition from child to woman. Anticipating a moment of awakening, when latent sexuality is actualised, the imagery of young girls invites a wedding – or a first seduction.

Wise brides pick maids with care!

e Lysette's pretty bridesmaids wearing nighties?

Mummy,
I'm going to be a
butiful princess!

That's good. Then you can
keep us in our old age.

But Daddy'll be
able to do that.

A touching faith in Daddy's infallibility.
And there are
same position
the wisdom of
Life Assuranc
families. The
all this mone
great benefit

Life Assuran
of fathers ev

Th
Daddy
a

Christine Cashman raises her crown after being voted Miss Pears 1979 in London yesterday. The four-year-old from South Croydon also won £1,000

What a difference a week makes!

MODEL: Michelle pictured on a fashion assignment last week.

SCHOOLGIRL model Michelle Cook didn't wear her gold sling-back sandals yesterday. They wouldn't have looked quite right with woolly socks and regulation school uniform.

Michelle 16, was just another name on Form 5B's register after a half-term holiday spent making headlines.

Friends

She became famous after her parents were fined £150 for allowing her to skip lessons to concentrate on the glamour business.

The law says Michelle must stay at school—Denefield Comprehensive in Reading, Berks—until Easter.

As she arrived at the gates, Michelle, of Dell Road, Reading, said:

"Last week was absolutely fantastic. It made me even more sure I want to be a professional model."

But she added: "I expect I'll get a bit of stick from my friends because some of them will be envious.

"Lots of girls of my age want to be models but not many get the chance."

Now that Michelle has a bright future on the catwalk — she is on the books of a London agency — she is not very keen on going back to school.

She said: "I'd rather not be there at all. I want to get away from classes as quickly as I can."

Pictures: JOHN PAUL and DAVID WHITE

PUPIL: Michelle at school yesterday

The popular press observes the transition with relish. Newspaper stories tell of teachers' disapproval as the young girl escapes the constriction of school uniform and enters a public world where men may openly respond to her sexuality. 'My figure has always brought a lot of comments,' said the sixteen-year-old Samantha Fox when her career was launched in 1983, 'so why not show it?' The *Star* followed a fifteen-year-old model in a series of pin-up pictures which despite protests, culminated in a topless pose on her sixteenth birthday. The visual transformation is a masculine triumph.

Relations of power through sexuality constantly challenge the boundary between girl child and adult woman. A game of provocation and denial, titillation and outrage, is played around the unstable division between the two. The word 'girl' can refer to a woman of any age, implying a continuation of her defenceless availability. The pin-up girl, the chorus girl, the girlfriend – a word which stands for a child in whom sexuality must be repressed also stands for a woman defined by her sexuality. But at the same time the word summons up childhood as a paradigm for dependency, vulnerability and subordination, and imputes those characteristics to the whole female group. In *Gender Advertisements*, Erving Goffman isolates the childish gestures typical of the women in the advertisements he studied – the finger on the lip, the unrestrained laughter, the childish glee. The domination/subordination relationship between men and women is paralleled and reinforced by the domination/subordination relationship between adults and children. The image of the child-woman balances that of the too-knowing child. In the first case, seductiveness seems an innocent condition of a woman's being which she does not choose and cannot reject; in the second, it may be openly displayed but its consummation is tabooed.

The paradoxical relations between childhood and femininity are explored in many different ways in popular imagery. One device is the salacious joke of the school uniform. Young women in uniform can turn sensible shoes into sexy ones, they can advertise 'men's' magazines, they can point fun at the 'prudes'. The uniform attempts to control bodies that refuse to be controlled. Breasts and buttocks burst out and insist that femininity will not be contained within the limits imposed by the institutions of childhood. Severe gymslips are lifted to reveal stocking tops, frilly knickers and suspenders. Forbidden parts of the body are indicated by old-fashioned underclothing that has itself become part of the stock in trade of pornography. The uniform brings with it the sado-masochistic fantasy of school as a place of sexualised discipline.

Clarks

Red Leather,   Yellow Leather,   Green Leather,   Brown Leather.

As concern over sexist upbringing has increased, and unisex clothing has become the norm, we have seen many pictures of confident little girls, usually aged around eight or nine, who look the camera in the eye with unembarrassed directness. But it needs only a slight adjustment, a tilt of the head to one side, to add a bashful self-awareness. Whatever her age, the imagery routinely bends the head of the young girl, sexualises her image, distinguishes her from the mischievous young boys who accompany her. It constantly

★
'Anchors
away!'

returns her to that transitional time when she is 'too old for toys, too young for boys'. Her face takes on a dreamy look, anticipating, dreading, that moment when a loss of innocence becomes a recognition of male potency. As a child, sexuality is forbidden to her, and it is that very ignorance that makes her the most perfect object of men's desire, the inexperienced woman. Thus the fascinating exchange between knowledge and ignorance reaches beyond the boundary between girl and woman and towards the forbidden

attraction of innocence itself, the sexuality of the child. The imagery of girl children balances childhood and femininity in contradiction and competition. Indications of sexuality which are too overt are either rejected or disavowed, and visual strategies which indicate childhood are always aware of the impossibility of separating femininity from sexuality. A little girl may be denied knowledge of sex, but as a feminine creature her *image* cannot fail to indicate sex.

This game of hide-and-seek has been played with different variations in the image of young girls over the last two decades. There has been an effort to push the explicit sexualisation of girl children to an ever younger age. A spate of American films at the end of the 1970s worked the genre pioneered by *Lolita* a decade earlier, and portrayed girl children whose loss of innocence made them openly seductive. At the age of twelve, Brooke Shields played a child prostitute in *Pretty Baby* (1977). At thirteen, Jodie Foster leaned provocatively against a lamppost in *Taxi Driver* (1976). Features about child stars recycled the image in the press and periodicals. In the distinction between actor and role, was innocence broken or preserved? Brooke Shields was bound by contract to remain a virgin until her twentieth birthday, and both girls were always accompanied by their mothers. When Jodie had just turned sixteen, the *Star* told us 'the baby is a vamp'. She had a 'thirty-year-old woman's mind in a child's body'. She was pictured sitting, legs apart, in the most openly sexual of poses, with a knowing awareness which dared the adult male to broach the taboo. Model agencies began seeking ever younger girls for adult poses. 'The more untouched the face, the better the model', a make-up artist told Victor Davis of the *Mail on Sunday*. Milla Jovovich, aged twelve, became the 'hottest new American fashion model', remarkable for the contrast between her siren's head and 'pre-nubile body'.

Ambiguous imagery of this sort is embedded in narratives of incredulity, suggestiveness or condemnation. The pictures are surrounded by a flow of words, grey lines of print, which attempt to hold them in place. 'Is there anybody in this country who really cares about our innocent children?' asked Barbara Jones in the *Mail on Sunday* of the relationship between fifty-year-old Rolling Stone Bill Wyman and thirteen-year-old Mandy Smith. 'To hear the story as I did from Mandy's own lips as she curled up childlike on the sofa in her mini-dress would bring tears to the eyes of any decent mother or father.' But the other side of Mandy's spoilt innocence was her assertiveness. She was presented as the archetypal 'bimbo' – a new, shameless breed of exploitative girl-women, the gold-diggers of 1986, setting a trap for wealthy middle-aged men.

What disturbs those viewers who feel that there is no security without hard-and-fast categories is that we can never really know, however hard we scrutinise their pictures and however often they are photographed, posing for the camera or candidly snapped, whether Mandy, Milla and all the others are only playing at adulthood, like every little girl, or whether they have in fact matured too young. As adulthood and childishness merge and blur, what

So, daddy please remember this,
That tomorrow starts a life of bliss,
Let me show them what they're gonna miss,
Kiss the boys goodbye.
'Kiss The Boys Good-bye', lyrics by Frank Loesser

varn you laddie,
u're perfectly swell,
elongs to daddy,
ly, he treats it so well.
elongs To Daddy', Lyrics by Cole Porter

55 Brompton Road, Knightsbridge, London S.W.3. Telephone: 01-584 8571 Telex: 21296

Graff
Unmistakably.

disturbs is the disappearance of the boundary. But when, in a rather different image, the child is decked out with the earrings, mascara and cigarette-holder of the sophisticated woman, the pictures are keeping the *concepts* of adulthood and childhood sharply separate, as their symbols are brought together in the frame. These little girls would not convey their ironic message if they did not retain the

You wouldn't do it to your baby.
We wouldn't do it to our babyfood.

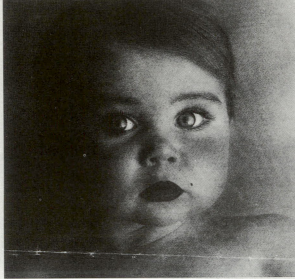

The make-up on this little girl's face contains no less than 100 chemicals.

It seems outrageous to do such a thing to her delicate baby skin. (And of course we didn't. We re-touched the photograph.)

But what about her delicate baby stomach?

It's quite within the law to add some 4,000 artificial additives to baby foods.

When you think about it, that's even more outrageous.

Young babies are particularly vulnerable to the adverse effects of artificial additives.

Because the mechanisms which provide protection against these substances are not fully developed.

For that reason, we'd like to tell you what we don't put in any Cow & Gate babyfood. Or juice. Or rusk. Or yogurt.

No artificial colouring.

Since when did a baby complain that our Vegetable Casserole and Pasta looked a bit on the pale and pasty side?

Or our Strawberry Fool looked a trifle dull?

The value of artificial colouring is purely cosmetic. And you all know what we think about that.

No artificial flavouring.

When we first mixed up our Lamb Dinner, we decided it wasn't as tasty as it could be.

But the last thing we thought of adding was artificial flavouring.

We simply added a few carrots.

That way we improved both the taste and nutritional value. And that's the way we make all our babyfoods.

No artificial preservatives.

Many manufacturers go along with adding artificial preservatives. Granted, that's one way of doing it.

We prefer to employ some 400 people checking, sterilising or pasteurising, double-checking, then vacuum sealing.

We even put a 'safety button' on baby-

meal jars. So you can check that the food is perfect condition.

No added salt.

Young babies don't have fully mature kidneys. If they are over-loaded with too much salt, it can build up in their blood. Besides that, the foods we use naturally contain any salt a baby needs.

So salt is one thing you'll never find in our tables.

No need to guess.

We want you to know exactly what goes into our babyfoods.

On every Cow & Gate label, there's a complete list of ingredients. Plus nutritional information.

In addition, the 'tick' system means each item can be checked for additives, at a glance.

If you'd like a leaflet that goes into even more detail, write to Consumer Affairs (G.N.), Cow & Gate, Trowbridge, Wiltshire BA14 8YX.

✓	NO ADDED SUGAR
	GLUTEN FREE
	NO ARTIFICIAL COLOURING
	NO ADDED PRESERVATIVES
✓	NO ARTIFICIAL FLAVOURING
	NO ADDED SALT
	ADDED VITAMIN C

Clearly, we shy away from the use of anything artificial. Only adding Vitamin C to our drinks. Or a tiny sprinkling of sugar to some of our fruit puddings. But only enough to overcome the natural tartness of the fruit.

So when you pop Cow & Gate food into a baby's mouth, you can be sure it's as natural as we can possibly make it.

Babies being babies, they may end up with their faces covered in food. But at least you know its not covered in artificial chemicals.

Baby meals. Baby Juices. Liga Rusks

unknowing freshness that we recognise as childhood itself. The device is pushed to its extreme with Cow and Gate's baby with full make-up on her face, which caused a stir in the advertising world in 1988. The agency, Abbott Mead Vickers/SMS, was at pains to point out that the effect was achieved by retouching a photograph – but the advertisement created what Tony Brignull, chair of the judges for the *Campaign* Press awards, described as 'that frisson of shock which is often the hallmark of great ads'. The two approaches play with the frisson around femininity and childishness in different ways. The image of the child who behaves like a woman, despite her childish qualities, draws attention to the impossibility of keeping the categories apart. The image of the child dressed up with all the sexuality of an adult woman demonstrates the impossibility of keeping them together.

But the question remains: Who is it that is playing these games with the images of young girls? Pictures which explicitly eroticise girl children continue to be circulated while scandals over child sexual abuse and child pornography escalate. A revulsion against the abuse of young girls can easily be extended to a revulsion at pictures said to encourage abuse. 'The use of children to imitate adult sexual behaviour sounds disgusting and would almost certainly be illegal' was the reply given by the Advertising Standards Authority to Women's Media Action in 1987 when they launched a campaign against the use of children dressed as adults. However, the ASA failed to ban the specific advertisements drawn to their attention.

Campaigns to preserve the purity of childhood risk turning their backs on precisely those areas most in need of a playful, if fearful, exploration. The little girl tottering on her high heels in front of the mirror is herself making sense and learning to make use of the role she is expected to play. An exploration of childhood sexuality and its rapid transformations will inevitably venture near the edge of what is acceptable. Pictures that even pose the question touch their viewers, female as well as male, in unexpected ways. The sense of transgression they bring is undoubtedly pleasurable in itself. Those who are shocked by such pictures may even seek them out for the satisfaction of condemning them.

A dominant reading continues to see such images as teasing the gaze of the adult male. But to retain that effect – and preserve their enticing quality – they, too, must protect the 'childishness' of children. Their interests are parallel to those who campaign for the purity of childhood and fear its loss. It may be, rather, that a loss of innocence is children's best protection against exploitation. The images themselves are a battleground for power and pleasure. Their meanings are taken, transformed, rearranged and reused, At some points the shocking suggestion that girls are passively available seems to dominate; at others it looks as if girls have the chance of taking their sexuality into their own hands. But girls remain vulnerable to dominant meanings. If they refuse to be treated as children, they can do so only on terms already laid down by society. 'I lead an adult life, but I won't throw childhood away,' said a fifteen-year-old model who admitted that she first had sex at thirteen. 'I'll still be a child at eighty and have Coco Pops for breakfast.'

Nevertheless, across the range from flirting bimbos down to pouting babies, we have been trained by the imagery itself to read all pictures of girls in an erotic way. The image of the sexy young woman teaches us how to interpret the ambiguous spectacle of the baby face or the mini-pin-up which is a regular feature of the daily press. The opportunity is taken up by the importers and manufacturers of postcards of cute and provocative children, boys as well as girls, who are credited to such sources as the Truly Scrumptious model agency. Their suggestiveness is disingenuously denied by their producers. 'Our minds don't work in that way', the sales manager of a postcard publishing company told Geraldine Bedell of the *Independent on Sunday*. She responded with an awareness characteristic of the 1990s: 'As soon as you are sensitised to the reactions of paedophiles you start to see unhealthy images of children where before you might only have seen cute ones.'

Resistance to the image is grist to the mill of the erotic, since masculine pleasure is partly defined as the overcoming of feminine resistance. Much of the attraction in pictures of young girls is the poignancy of those charming and impotent efforts to delay the inevitable. The childhood of girls is like an unfinished narrative; the unresolved potential holds readers in its thrall. Impediments and detours only intensify its delights.

Theresa Bennett, aged 12, limbers up for her battle for equal rights on the football field.

The image of the tomboy is one such delay, its significance sharpened by its hopelessness. The period is so short before the girl must give up her deluded aspirations and become fixed in her femininity. Occasionally there are newspaper stories of girls who excel at football or some other male preserve, but are barred from the team or club because of their sex. The tragedy is in their brief delusion that they may escape. In our available imagery the mischievous imp leaping with the boys and joining in with the gang needs only a change of clothing to become once more the soulful waif in Victorian knickers.

However, there is always more than one way of understanding a picture, and the narrative tells quite a different story when looked at with the eyes not of the controlling male, but of the inventive and assertive girl herself. Even so, playing with their image is a risky business for young girls as they balance welcome pleasures with dubious pressures. 'We speak their language, they respond,' IPC told advertisers of its young women's magazines. 'Romance is here. Your message can reach her at her most receptive.' Adolescent femininity is responsive. It is about living for the moment and for a future made up of similar moments: 'Today is what you make it. Tomorrow will be even better.' The passage from childhood is eased by fun; making up, dressing up, romping with all the abandon of a bunch of eight-year-olds. Advertising for teenage girls shows them in each other's company, enjoying a night on the town. The potential male partner has not yet imposed his restraints.

But this bubbling sexuality, if not kept in check, may well burst forth in the disaster of unwanted babies, teenage prostitutes and corrupted adolescents. This alternative image of the young girl is regularly made available in the popular press. She sits, often head in hands, slouched and unkempt. We are forcibly reminded that she is no longer alluring once she is degraded by prostitution or becomes a gymslip mother. In such cases the transformation from child to adult may be presented in punitive terms. 'Thirty-six hours in labour, which is common, changed them dramatically', said the principal of a school for teenage mothers.

By the mid 1980s, the views of Mary Whitehouse, Victoria Gillick and other moral purity campaigners had gained a new credibility as the backlash against 'permissiveness' gained momentum and the advent of AIDS introduced new cautions. AIDS made it possible to

speak of sex to young people, but as a danger not as a pleasure. Sex education in schools has been at the centre of recurring disputes. In the view of Mary Whitehouse, too much knowledge deprives children of their innocence and, indeed, of childhood itself. The image of the young girl, with all its ambiguities, remains at the centre of all discussions of childhood sexuality. Her potential and her very presence introduce a disturbance into demands for purity and control. However repressive the text that surrounds her picture, however strong the call for parents to assert their authority and for society to return to traditional values, her image continues to generate excitement. 'How young is too young for love?' newspapers continuously demand. 'If kisses were not forbidden in school,' said one headmaster, 'twelve- and thirteen-year-olds would be making love in the corridors.'

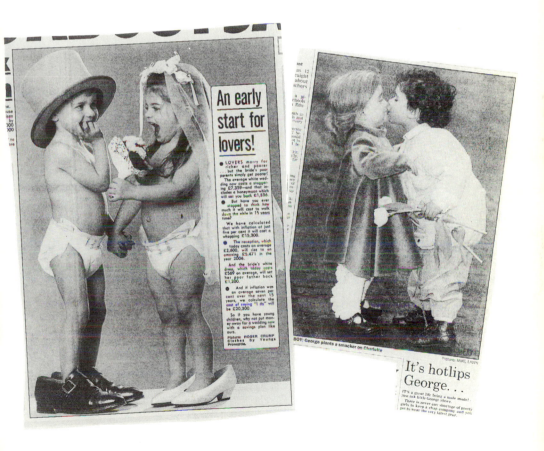

An early start for lovers!

● LOVERS marry for richer and poorer... but the bride's poor parents simply get poorer!

The average white wedding now costs a staggering £7,359—and that includes a honeymoon which will set you back £1,936.

● But have you ever stopped to think how much it will cost to walk down the aisle in 15 years' time?

We have calculated that with inflation at just five per cent it will cost a whopping £15,300.

● The reception, which today costs on average £2,600, will rise to an amazing £5,471 in the year 2006.

And the bride's white dress, which today costs £509 on average, will set her poor father back £1,200.

● And if inflation was seven per cent over the next 15 years, we calculate the cost of saying "I do" will be £20,300.

So if you have young children, why not put money away for a wedding now with a savings plan like ours.

Picture: ROGER CRUMP
Clothes by Younger Promotions.

BOY: George plants a smacker on Charlotte

Picture: MIKE LAWN

It's hotlips George...

IT'S a great life being a male model just ask little George above.

There is never any shortage of pretty girls to keep a chap company and you get to wear the very latest gear.

The image of the girl-woman holds yet another threat to masculinity and the male position. Not only are men seduced into transgression by the impossible innocence of the feminine, but young males are themselves in danger of being feminised by their relation to adult male power. In *The Best Kept Secret*, Florence Rush argues that the social bisexuality of children is female rather than male, since both boys and girls stand in the same relation to adult men. In public imagery boys, too, may be presented as soft and attractive.

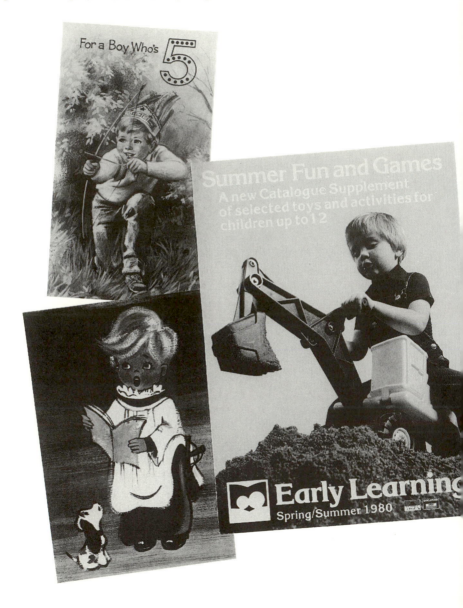

The taboos that surround boyhood sexuality are, if anything, even stronger than those around girls. Passivity and softness are feminising; sexual assertiveness poses a dangerous challenge to adult men. The gamin image of a boy, with the soulful expression more often found on a girl, is cautiously used on birthday cards or advertisements. Much more frequently, advertisements in particular call on all the symbols of power to render sexuality itself invisible and reassert the position of the boy as the inheritor of the dominant position of the adult male. Boys are much more likely to distress, threaten or judge their mothers. Their choice of toys involves tools, machines and weapons. They are rarely shown in repose. Instead they run, leap, throw, climb or engage in effective activity. The image of the young toughie becomes the regular face of boyhood. His knowingness is a cheeky naughtiness; his angelic face is belied by the catapult in his pocket. The image of the boy is strongly defended against sexuality and feminisation.

A Tough Act to Follow. That's Asda Style.

Comfortable shapes, bright splashes of colour. That's Kids Klobber, at Asda now.

SWEATSHIRT £6.99 ▲ GILET £5.99 ▲ JOGPANTS £5.99 ▲ HAT AND SCARF SET £3.99

ZIP NECK SWEATSHIRT £6.99 ▲ JOGPANTS £5.99 ▲ BRIGHT SOCKS (2 PR. PACK) £1.49

Asda

7

Crybabies and damaged children

Save the children?

Without the image of the unhappy child, our contemporary concept of childhood would be incomplete. Real children suffer in many different ways and for many different reasons, but pictures of sorrowing children recall those defining characteristics of childhood: dependence and powerlessness.

Children living in poverty, children suffering from neglect or disadvantage, children who are the victims of wars or natural disasters – they figure in imagery as the most vulnerable, the most pathetic, the most deserving of all of our sympathy and aid. They are on the receiving end of an oppression in which they can only acquiesce. Children are seen as archetypal victims; childhood is seen as weakness itself. As the children in the image reveal their vulnerability, we long to protect them and provide for their needs. Paradoxically, while we are moved by the image of a sorrowful child, we also welcome it, for it can arouse pleasurable emotions of tenderness, which in themselves confirm adult power.

As with children, so with all those other groups who bear the characteristics of childhood – women, Black people and the whole of the Third World are among those who stand in a childish relation to the exercise of power. The non-white nations are regularly presented as if in themselves they lack potency, and it is among the children of the developing countries – in stark contrast to the well-fed, well-equipped mini-consumers of the domestic image – that we find the most frequent pictures of childhood suffering.

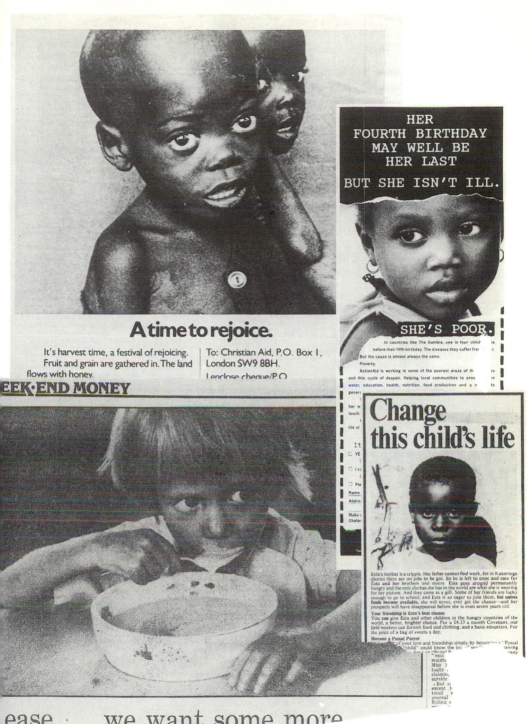

A time to rejoice.

It's harvest time, a festival of rejoicing. Fruit and grain are gathered in. The land flows with honey.

To: Christian Aid, P.O. Box 1, London SW9 8BH.

I enclose cheque/P.O.

HER
FOURTH BIRTHDAY
MAY WELL BE
HER LAST

BUT SHE ISN'T ILL.

SHE'S POOR.

In countries like The Gambia, one in four children die before their fifth birthday. The diseases they suffer from, but the cause is almost always the same. Poverty.

ActionAid is working in some of the poorest areas of the end this cycle of despair. Helping local communities to prov water, education, health, nutrition, food production and a n

EEK·END MONEY

Change this child's life

Esta's mother is a cripple. Her father cannot find work, for in Kakemega district there are no jobs to be got. So he is left to cope and care for Esta and her brothers and sisters. Esta goes around permanently hungry and the only clothes she has in the world are what she is wearing for her picture. And they came as a gift. Some of her friends are lucky enough to go to school, and Esta is so eager to join them, but unless funds become available, she will never, ever get the chance—and her prospects will have disappeared before she is even seven years old.

Your friendship is Esta's best chance
You can give Esta and other children in the hungry countries of the world, a better, brighter chance. For a £4.33 a month Covenant, our field workers can furnish food and clothing, and a basic education. For the price of a bag of sweets a day.

Become a Postal Parent

ease ... we want some more

including Dr Barnado's, may provide the answer. As joint sponsors of the

tions even though the usual provisions insist that there be a

the fund yet at a Mer

The one area where the British image industry regularly and predictably produces pictures of Black and other non-white children is in press reports of wars, famine and natural disasters and in the appeals for aid which accompany such reports. The wide eyes of the needy dark-skinned child look reproachfully out from news pages and from those advertisements that solicit rather than seduce. The ragged child who is not ashamed to plead so dominates the available imagery of Africa, Latin America and the Indian subcontinent that the whole of that vast area beyond Western culture seems in itself to be a place of distress and childish subservience. Third World suffering acts to secure our sense of First World comfort by assuring us that we have the power to help. That power is confirmed by the gaze of an appealing child, carefully selected so that it in no way undermines our complacent certainty of our own position. These pictured children are not refugees challenging our borders; they are not armed guerrillas causing international disruption; they are without the stench of disease which might make their physical presence repellent. Their humble and submissive appeal protects our compassion and enables us to give.

In the act of looking at these presentations, viewers recognise themselves as both adult and Western, as individuals with the ability to change a child's life for the better without changing their own for the worse. The only possible relationship for this pictured child is with the putative viewer. The Black child is seeking a white benefactor, a surrogate parent who will be more effective than his own absent Black parent. The appeal is to the competence of Western civilisation, seen not as the controlling father, imposing the harsh disciplines of international finance, but as the nurturing mother, the Mother Countries. He looks to the First World as his only source of help and succour: Be my postal parent! Help me!

Over the last twenty years the increased accessibility of information in words and pictures in the press and on television has made war, famine, drought and disasters of cataclysmic proportions familiar parts of our everyday consciousness. From the worsening famine in the Sahel region of Northern Africa and the increasingly serious floods and cyclones in the Indian subcontinent, to the wars which have devastated Lebanon, Cambodia, East Timor, Iraq and many other parts of the globe, pictures which document natural disasters have formed a continuum with those which show the results of human atrocity. In the filtering and selection processes which lead to a decision about which picture will make the front page, and which photographer will become photographer of the year, attention is consistently directed towards those whose hardship is greatest. Children have remained at the centre of the image.

As familiarity has blunted their effectiveness, pictures of suffering have become less restrained. If they are not sufficiently shocking, photographs will not break through the news barrier and on to the front pages. 'It's an unfortunate truism of famines, that by the time the pictures are horrific enough to move people, it's almost too late', wrote journalist and film-maker Paul Harrison. The Western public has become familiar with an imagery of extremity at the expense of context, and the wrenching of emotion at the expense of understanding.

The implicit question that runs through the imagery of distress which has echoed between aid advertisements and the news pages is: Who can take responsibility for the child?

The pictures can be read as a series of reflections on that problem. A frequent image is that of mother and child together, the weakness of the mother serving only to intensify the plight of the child. Her breasts are drained dry, she cannot fulfil the only role that justifies her presence. The total ineffectuality of the Third World mother was brought home by a picture which made the front page of several

AN THIRD WORLD REVIEW

rying need is for political cour

28 January

7   The Ra
     Cove

10   Prelu
     Four
     in no
     harve

18   It's a
     The
     once
     Dene
     and g
     and gr

28   The Rer
     Six of
     were
     Rent
     them

34   Some
     The
     sile
     no
     w
     b
     t

42   T

A woman with her severely malnourished baby in northern Ethiopia. Photographed by Stuart Nicol. See page 10.

mpson photographed in Aspen by Eric Lars R

In rural Bangladesh the gap between the medical establishment and the people is still as wide as ever

lenders do wonders for the   train   65,000   "village   have difficulty in serving in   under the programme lived family's health chart   doctors," each comple

Who can save us?

● IT ISN'T a doll being cuddled in the arms of this sad-faced little girl — it's her baby brother, and he's just a few hours from death.

● The wafer-thin tot and his hollow-eyed sister are among 10 million people dying of disease and famine in cyclone-devastated Bangladesh. Baby Jibon was born at the height of the horror. Ironically, his name means "life".

● But, by the time you read this, he will most probably be dead.

Crisis in Bangladesh — Turn to Page 2

national dailies after the cyclone which devastated parts of Bangladesh in May 1991. A child was forced to play mother, cradling her baby brother in her arms.

Men are rarely visible in the iconography of disaster. It is they who signify culture, and whose presence tends to locate a picture in its geographical context. They are more likely to be fully clothed or to be engaged in some task. As the strongest group they are least likely to conform to the expected image of the victim and the most likely to be involved in attempts at reconstruction or resistance, confusing the clarity of the story, complicating a reaction of pity alone. Thus the community to which the suffering child belongs is visually bypassed, and the extent to which it is caring for its own children is rarely explored.

The aid agencies – Oxfam, Save the Children, Christian Aid and others – have been closest to events in disaster-prone areas, and have frequently led the news media. In 1973 Oxfam brought back the first pictures of the Ethiopian famine, and in 1991 a group of agencies

arranged for journalists to tour parts of Africa that would otherwise
have dropped out of media consciousness. But in their advertising
they have had to balance the need for information which bears the
full complexity of a situation against the need to penetrate the
everyday parade of consumer images with presentations that will
encourage people to give. Their approach has changed since Oxfam
captioned a desperate mother and child in a 1970s advertisement:
'Please sir, I beseech you, give me something for my baby.' By the
early 1980s pleading had given way to shock tactics. 'Unless shown
the full horror of a situation, few people are sufficiently moved to
give', said the *Guardian* in 1982. For a while it seemed as if only the
most extreme image would compel an uncaring public to pay
attention.

While you're eating between meals, he's dying between meals.

We thought that we should never again be forced to show you a picture like this. But the plight of thousands of starving children demands that we must.
All over the world, children are dying for want of food. For food, we need money. For money, Save the Children is looking to you.
You can save a child from death as surely as if you were out there with the Save the Children teams. One pound will feed one of our children for a week.

Give what you can. Your money can never buy anything more precious than a child's life.

Please accept my donation of _____ (National Giro No. 517 3000)
Name _____
Address _____

Please tick only if you require a receipt ☐

STM/M

Save the Children
The Save the Children Fund, 157 Clapham Road, London SW9 0PT

Both Oxfam and Save the Children used pictures of the emaciated
bodies of children, surely only hours from death, against a stark
white background. These posters appeared in shocking juxtaposition
with the minutiae of everyday life in the pages of magazines and on
hoardings above city streets. Unlike the children in the wide-eyed
image, these children could not fix the viewers with their reproachful
gaze.

The relationship between the dying Black child and the viewing
white adult was one of guilt by comparison. 'You are eating while he
is dying' . . . 'Your weight problems are different from his' . . .

forcing the viewer to use text as only context. In the absence of more
visual information, the power of interpretation is left with the
controlling white eye outside the frame. In some advertisements,
succouring white hands appeared to support or feed the emaciated
child. The image operated in a dangerous area between sympathy,
guilt and disgust. In abandoning the attractiveness of childhood,
these pictured children may well have sacrificed the indulgence
childhood commands. Without the flattery offered by the appealing
image they may arouse adult sadism without deflecting it and
confirm a contempt for those many parts of the world which seem
unable to help their own. For there was a tendency to generalise the
appeal: 'All over the world children are dying for want of food' . . .
'Over vast areas of the earth, in the poor lands of Africa, Asia, and
Latin America, harvests have failed or are inadequate' . . . By the late
1980s the use of this sort of image was coming under attack from
people in the developing countries, from Black and Asian British
people and from photographers who were not satisfied with the way
their work was being used. They argued that an imagery that
stressed helplessness and dependence fuelled racism, and affected
the way not just Third World people but *all* non-white people were
perceived.

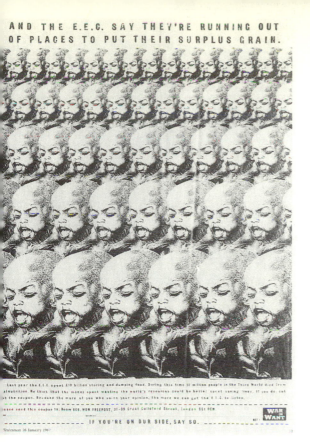

AND THE E.E.C. SAY THEY'RE RUNNING OUT OF PLACES TO PUT THEIR SURPLUS GRAIN.

Last year the E.E.C. spent £10 billion storing and dumping food. During this time 17 million people in the Third World died from malnutrition. We think that the money spent wasting the world's resources could be better spent saving lives. If you do, cut out the coupon. Because the more of you who voice your opinion, the more we can get the E.E.C. to listen.

please send this coupon to: Room 808, WON FREEPOST, 37-39 Great Guildford Street, London SE1 0EN.

IF YOU'RE ON OUR SIDE, SAY SO.

WAR ON WANT

Statesman 16 January 1987

Meanwhile, in campaigning publications, the image of the starving child had been used to produce a different kind of explanation. Instead of the context of supportive Western aid, these presentations placed the child amongst the symbols of Western exploitation – the baby-milk bottle, the canned food, the roll of film. The relationship of unequal trade and accumulating debt between First and Third World countries led to what Teresa Hayter called the 'grotesque hypocrisy' of the rich countries' claim to 'help the Third World escape the poverty which they and their predecessors partly created and continue to create'. In 1985 the United Nations Children's Fund attacked the World Bank, the International Monetary Fund and other financial institutions for 'imposing draconian austerity measures in the name of economic adjustment' on some of the world's poorest countries, and thereby endangering many children. With this analysis in mind, War on Want ran a series of advertisements, using drawings rather than photographs, which set out to make explicit links between Third World poverty and Third World debt, commenting in one on the dreadful repetition of images of starving children. The 'Bogeyman' campaign was very successful, but the charitable status of the agencies means that they risk censure by the Charity Commissioners when their message is overtly political. The strategy has been instead

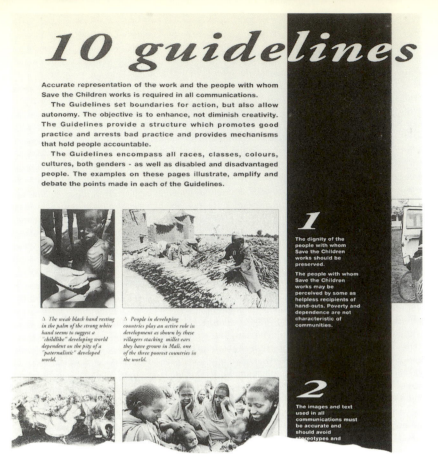

10 guidelines

Accurate representation of the work and the people with whom Save the Children works is required in all communications.

The Guidelines set boundaries for action, but also allow autonomy. The objective is to enhance, not diminish creativity. The Guidelines provide a structure which promotes good practice and arrests bad practice and provides mechanisms that hold people accountable.

The Guidelines encompass all races, classes, colours, cultures, both genders - as well as disabled and disadvantaged people. The examples on these pages illustrate, amplify and debate the points made in each of the Guidelines.

△ *The weak black hand resting in the palm of the strong white hand seems to suggest a "childlike" developing world dependent on the pity of a "paternalistic" developed world.*

△ *People in developing countries play an active role in development as shown by these villagers stacking millet ears they have grown in Mali, one of the three poorest countries in the world.*

1

The dignity of the people with whom Save the Children works should be preserved.

The people with whom Save the Children works may be perceived by some as helpless recipients of hand-outs. Poverty and dependence are not characteristic of communities.

2

The images and text used in all communications must be accurate and should avoid stereotypes and

to look for 'positive images' and 'accuracy' of representation. In 1991 Save the Children's published guidelines for photographers were based on the principle that 'the dignity of the people with whom Save the Children works should be preserved . . . portraying poverty and dependence as the norm is not accurate . . . The people with whom Save the Children works risk "exploitation by camera" if their identity or opinions are excluded in the promotion of development issues.'

Nevertheless, the dilemma remains. At a time when the public is said to be suffering from 'compassion fatigue', raising funds and raising awareness can seem like contradictory aims. Too much information can confuse the power of the image as understanding takes over from emotional response. Save the Children's advertising agency, Ogilvy and Mather, told the *Guardian*: 'Images of starving children have lost their appeal' at the same time as J. Walter Thompson, for Oxfam, insisted that 'a child will bring in more than an adult, a girl child who cries will bring in more than a boy who does not'. Save the Children call it a 'healthy tension'.

But the use of a child both in the press and in advertisements refers to a value that claims to be beyond explanation and outside politics. Children may express emotions that are universal while remaining separate from those other qualities that make humanity so diverse. Not yet fully participant in divisions of language, nationality, culture or even race, the child is presented as uncontaminated by their antagonistic forms. As the symbol of common humanity, a child may be the bearer of suffering with no responsibility for its causes. This view is in stark contrast to the practice of the starving nations, where the child is the most expendable. 'If a parent dies the family is doomed. The father eats first and dies last; the children eat last and die first', wrote Richard Dowden of the aid camps in Ethiopia. The irony of the aid imagery, then, is that however accurate the picture, an appeal on behalf of the children may necessarily be *against* the community of which they are part, rather than on that community's behalf. Since their community has failed them, the children need to be saved. They may be given a Western education, removed, adopted or even airlifted out. Children 'rescued' from the perceived disorder of the Third World are seen in the imagery with a symbol of the 'civilisation' they have reached – they clutch a teddy bear or stroke a dog.

For the popular press, the answer to the problem of who is responsible for the children is that civilisation is responsible, but can be effective only through charismatic individuals, like Bob Geldof or Mother Teresa or dramatic acts of charity. These are the factors that can turn a slow-developing disaster, like the famine in Ethiopia, into a newsworthy event. '*Mirror* to the rescue' was the headline to a picture story in October 1984. 'The *Daily Mirror* acted last night to boost the relief effort to Ethiopia's starving millions . . .' The newspapers seek to bring about a visual transformation – as with the Bangladeshi girl and her baby brother, rephotographed five days later by the *Daily Mail*: 'We brought them food, medicine and clothes . . . it brought a smile to the face of the little girl . . .'

FACE OF HOPE

The Mail brings comfort to the cyclone children

EXCLUSIVE From RICHARD KAY in Ghoramora, Bangladesh

THEIR tiny, helpless faces burned a haunting image on the consciousness of the West.

A little girl, wretched in the mud and clutching her baby brother like a broken doll, symbolised the terrible suffering of the Bangladesh cyclone victims when their picture was published around the world last week.

Yesterday, after a journey across a landscape of monsoons, past rivers of homeless and hungry, we found Shibarani Jaladaz, six, and the baby, now 16 days old and named Jibon, meaning life, because of his remarkable survival story. The family were still struggling to stay alive.

We brought them food, medicine and clothes. It wasn't much; rice for their meals, seed for the ground, some fruit, bread, and the means to restart some sort of life. It will help them survive for three months. But in a place where survival is measured by the day, it verged on the luxurious.

Chaotic

It brought a smile to the face of the little girl, tears to the eyes of her parents and hope to baby Jibon, whom we had expected to find already dead.

He was born just 48 hours before the cyclone tore across the Bay of Bengal 14 nights ago, blowing away his family's home and sparing only the clothes they were wearing.

Now his skin is waxen and his breath rasping and irregular. He is a scrap of a thing, probably weighing no more than a couple of bags of sugar. That he lived so long in a country where two babies die every minute is remarkable enough. Still more so as the family had had no food for five days before our arrival.

We found them in the ruins of the village of Ghoramora, an hour's drive from the port

Tragic: How we saw them on May 8

of Chittagong, with their father, Umakanta Jaladaz, 35, and his 28-year-old wife. They had left a chaotic evacuation centre to tramp back to where their home once stood. Now it was as though a giant had stepped on the place.

Their story is a snapshot of the disaster they called 'the will of Allah', which by last night had claimed almost 140,000 lives. On a

Turn to Page 3, Col. 1

Transformed: Shibarani cradling Jibon yesterday

Picture: FREDDY RIKKEN

An iconography of rescue forms an important part of the imagery of childhood, as we see pictures of children being brought out of earthquakes, fires and the rubble of war, or simply being found when lost. In Third World imagery, the role of the rescuer tends to be played by supportive white representatives of a technologised civilisation – doctors, nurses, aid workers. When the narrative of rescue takes place in Britain, even though the community is seen as responsible, professional rescuers, apart from the police, are seldom praised. Representatives of the soft state – social workers, NHS doctors, charity officials – tend to be treated with attitudes that range from suspicion to outright abuse. In the domestic iconography of rescue, technology plays an important role.

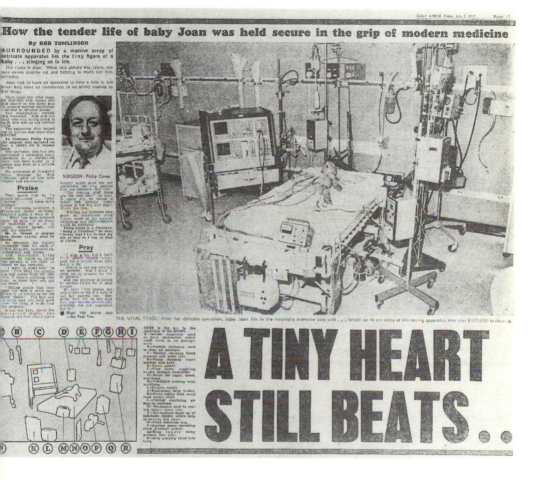

SUNDAY Mirror

June 1, 1986   FORWARD WITH BRITAIN   28p

CHILDREN OF WAR

IN place of toys they are given Kalashnikov rifles. In place of childhood they face death or mutilation.

They are the child warriors in a world scarred by more than 20 wars.

Clasping their deadly hardware they stare out of the page. Some manage a wan smile, others display the haunted eyes of battle-weary soldiers.

Many have not reached their teens, yet they are considered old enough to fight and die for causes of which they can have no conception.

In Afghanistan, in Iraq, in Kampuchea and in Lebanon their innocence has been torn away by the generals and the politicians.

The insignia these children wear is a badge of shame for the world.

● TURN TO CENTRE PAGES

Afghanistan—Abdul Ali, 12, taken from his parents for army training.

Kampuchea—a boy soldier in the Khmer Rouge guerrilla army.

Leban... ...as ab...

CHILDREN IN CONFLICT
MORRIS FRASER

Children at arms . . . youngsters prepare for graduation to the ranks of the rebel Sudan People's Liberation Army.

The child who appeals to the viewer, humbly requesting help, has remained the mainstay of aid imagery. But children's actual response to conditions of deprivation may well refuse qualities of childhood which give them their pathos. It is less easy to deal with the image of children who have become fighters, workers or brutalised dwellers on the streets. In 1990 the United Nations estimated that 200,000 children under fifteen are bearing arms around the world, most of them in rebel armies. The image of a child with a gun has carried the ambivalent meanings of resistance to oppression by children fighting alongside their elders, as well as the exploitation and corruption of children by those elders. It moves from the extreme of the violent child out of control to that of the disciplined young person playing their part in an organised force.

Although the practice is common in many parts of the world, pictures of children at work under conditions of forced labour and with minimal wages have rarely found a place in available imagery – despite the efforts of organisations like the Anti-Slavery Society to expose such scandals as the carpet industry in India. By contrast, the image of the street urchin has an uneasy presence within travel imagery. The packaging of the people of other nations for the Western tourist has long included an element of sexual tourism. Tour guides have sections on red-light districts, and certain parts of the world – for example, Sri Lanka and Thailand – are known to be places where child prostitutes operate. The engaging impudence of the street-urchin image carries overtones of both sexuality and children's contribution to the tourist economy of those states. But it needs only a slight shift of perspective to see the child on the streets as an undesirable vagrant.

THE INDEPENDENT ON SUNDAY 2 MAY 1994 21

INSIDE STORY

Destitute children in São Paulo. In this country 27 million, mostly black, children live below the poverty line and popular prejudices abound against the poor, homeless young

The child murderers of Rio

Corpses have become a common sight in

WHEN you change money at Rio de

wealthy businessman from São Paulo asked me whether I really believed in ...

answer and anyway, we didn't among us left ...

For many years the Western media have made spasmodic reports on the street children of Latin America. They attracted mild international scandal, but seen from the distance of a continent could easily be made light of. But to many 'respectable' inhabitants of Rio and Bogotá such children are like garbage, spoiling the attractiveness of the city, as they pester tourists and rob respectable citizens. By 1990 there were reports that street children were being routinely murdered by semi-official death squads. In Rio such killings were said to be 'socially acceptable'. 'When you talk about Brazilian children you must understand that they are not the same as European children. They really are savages here. Most of the time they are killing *each other*', a Brazilian businessman told Zoe Heller of the *Independent on Sunday*. The high-circulation Rio daily *O Povo* is filled with photographs of mutilated corpses. Sometimes these are the only record of the deaths of children who have no parents, no birth certificates, no official existence. But that most shocking of images is by no means confined to Third World children.

'The victimisation of children is nowhere forbidden', wrote Alice Miller in *Thou Shalt Not Be Aware*. 'What is forbidden is to write about it.' Imagery, sometimes the most extreme imagery, can put together meanings that words hesitate to admit. Childhood is about impotence and weakness. Acceptable victimisation is part of the visual repertoire with which the concept of childhood crosses and influences the concepts of race and class. Starving child from the Third World or helpless child from the domestic imagery of poverty, the image of the child as victim prepares the way for an open expression of adult hatred and cruelty.

Tempting abuse

Tears are remarkable in men, expected in women, but part of the very condition of childhood. They are the only bodily fluid that may legitimately flow in public, and the less an individual aspires to power, the less they need restrain them. Normal childhood tears are under adult control. Easily provoked by a slap or a prohibition, they seem like an inevitable part of the relationship of training and care within which adults and children are entwined. Children will behave badly and adults will lose their temper, it's only to be expected. So we tend to judge pictures of distress in the light of our adult experience, repressing uneasy promptings from our childhood selves. Pictures in which tearfulness is comfortingly confined to children – and, what is more, where the tears are in the child's own interest – can only be reassuring. It is not only our children but our childhood we are firmly keeping in place. Pictures of weeping

Daily Mirror

BRITAIN'S BIGGEST DAILY SALE

3p Tuesday, September 19, 1972   No. 21,362

THANK GOD WE LIVE HERE?

Every ten minutes an act of criminal violence happens in this country

SHOCK ISSUE

A child weeps ... her face crumpled by unhappiness and fear. Her tears symbolise the agony of our present age of growing violence.

PLEASE TURN TO PAGE TWO

children are often reproduced purely for adult gratification – on postcards, as examples of art photography or as anonymous symbols of misery itself.

Yet tears may also be evidence of irrational adults, of harshly punitive relations, of a discipline which has run out of control. They may be evidence of neglect, cruelty or adult hatred. The viewer of the picture may be required to make an unwelcome identification and see the image from the perspective of the child who is suffering instead of that of the adult who may relieve that suffering. Our reluctance to take this step is clear from a range of imagery that is remarkably narrow and repetitive. Pictures of suffering children rarely allow their subjects to express any autonomy or resistance, but some presentations show bodies which are utterly crushed, and visibly distinguishable from the justly punished child by the weight of misery bearing down on them. They cover their faces as if sharing the shame of their situation. Viewers are invited to support these children against the adults who harmed them and find that they may do so without bringing their own hatred into question. For this image is intended to be read not as the normal consequence of relations between adults and children, but as evidence of cruel and unsuitable adults.

Yet these children, crouched or slumped, are rejected not only by the events which created their situation but also by the image which seeks to represent their plight. Once more, there is a certain satisfaction for adults in imagining such rejection – the getting rid or spitting out of unpleasant and unwanted elements. Childhood and the residues of its devastating emotions are amongst those things we would dearly love to expel, but obstinately remain part of our very selves. We are left with the possibility of crushing those unwelcome aspects of our selves, of beating them down, just like the child in the image. The slumped child, itself a temptation to adult violence, may become disgusting to us.

From babyhood, children are handled by their parents and carers. Parents retain the right to caress or chastise, and to exercise a discipline modulated by these two extremes. The adult touch restrains and controls the child in a way that gives sensuous pleasure to the toucher. But the point where gestures of control become unwelcome to the child and merge into the infliction of physical pain is uncertain. In Britain parents have clung to their right to punish their children by slapping or hurting them. A campaign which aimed to discourage such practices, launched in 1989 by a group of parents and teachers, was received with outrage by many, including the tabloid press. Parents, it was said, would be deprived of rights over their children, and children would be deprived of a firm upbringing at a time when they are too young to understand what is good for them.

In a much more shocking set of images, adult power over children's bodies has been pushed to the extreme. Until recently these had been the most secret of pictures, available only to the medical and judicial professions. They show children whose bodies do not merely express sorrow or despair but who, like the street children of Rio, have been mutilated and tortured. The pictures show the broken objects of extreme abuse.

From the 1970s onwards new histories of childhood have been written in Britain and the United States. Beatrice and Ronald Gross's *The Children's Rights Movement* was a libertarian polemic; Lloyd de Mause's *The History of Childhood* argued that historical changes are brought about by 'psychogenic factors'; Alice Miller's *Thou Shalt Not Be Aware* was written by a practising psychoanalyst who came to doubt the validity of psychoanalysis itself. All told a history of violence and oppression. 'The history of childhood is a nightmare

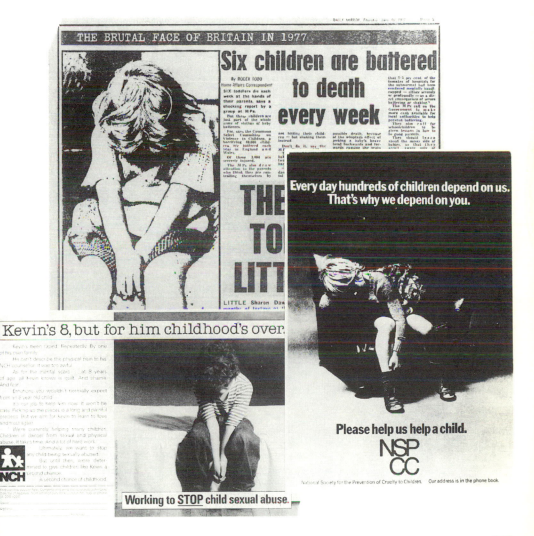

from which we have only recently begun to awaken', began de Mause. These authors describe habitual infanticide, mutilation, swaddling and other forms of restraint, enforced child labour, canings and beatings, sexual abuse and mental cruelty. They are catalogues of children's sufferings over the years at the hands of adults. 'Child abuse is so common that it may be a characteristic that comes close to being "natural" to the human condition', wrote D. Bakan in *The Slaughter of the Innocents*. At the same time, he argued, it is so terrible that subterfuges must be found to make it expressible. 'Hard thoughts which would be too unpleasant to think' underlie fantasy and fairy stories. 'There they are held fast in a frame of unbelief. Some things are simply too terrible to think about if one believes them. Thus one does not believe them in order to make it possible to think about them.'

Public narratives of child abuse which have escalated over the last decade reflect the fear associated with this image – the fear the strong have of the weak and the fear that excessive use of power leads not to control but to uncontrol, not to the overcoming of childhood but to a return to a childish lack of restraint. The damaged body of a child stands as evidence not of the child's painful accession to adult reason but of the unreasoning violence that adulthood cannot leave behind.

The narratives of the 1980s presented a world full of danger to children, who have been seen as constantly at risk. Stories of children who have gone missing or been murdered, raped and assaulted have been frequent. Many are illustrated with pictures – often snapshots or school photographs – of very ordinary little girls and boys. With hindsight, their tentative or confidently smiling faces acquire a dreadful poignancy. Childhood always looks nervously forward to an unknown future. For these children, the future has proved too terrible to contemplate. Their foolish confidence warns us that what happened to them may happen to any unwary child, so children are taught to beware of the danger from a stranger. But as the decade progressed, it became clear that those who threaten children include those closest to them. Recurring scandals have centred on girls who have died from injuries inflicted by their fathers or stepfathers: Maria Colwell in 1973, Tyra Henry in 1984, Jasmine Beckford in 1985, Kimberley Carlile in 1986 are only the most prominent amongst hundreds of cases, only some of which have been reported in the press. Since the report of the Committee of Inquiry into the death of Maria Colwell, there has been at least one major inquiry into a case of child abuse each year.

This harsh image was not the work of a stranger, nor could it be blamed on the children running wild in the streets. It was evidence of damage caused by the child's own protectors in the child's own home. Yet despite universal condemnation of such brutality, the concern of the popular press – and indeed of a large section of the social work profession – has been to defend the autonomy of the family group. The tabloids continue to seek dangers from without rather than disintegration from within. Even so, such extremity unlocks the heavily defended space of the family to a wide range of professionals. The Home Office Chief Medical Officer listed them in a publication in 1972: 'The local medical committee, paediatricians, consultants responsible for accident departments, the police, and social agencies such as the NSPCC'. These are impersonal officials and agents who appear to deal not with the child as a person, whose identity is confirmed by belonging to a family, but with the child's body as evidence and in need of repair. The medical and forensic image does not show the expression on the face or the expressivity of the body. The subjectivity of the child appears irrelevant to this relentless documentation. Thus, in the popular press, agents of the welfare state who aimed to protect children from abusing parents have joined the ranks of those outsiders who threaten the healing powers of the family itself. They have been condemned in tones which put the rescuers on a par with the abusers.

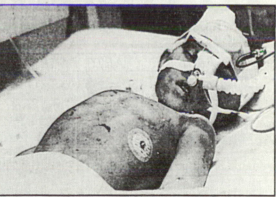

We can't take away the pain this child has been through. But with your help, we'll do our best to make sure it never happens to her again.
For the past hundred years, the NSPCC has been giving aid and comfort to abused children using your donations.

Her father bruised, burnt and broke her arm. Now we want to twist yours.

Last year, over 43,000 children relied on us for help.

enary and the[...]
reduction in t[...] need help.

THE GU

ich condemns the failures of social services and [...]

Anything[...] provide hel[...] even for as li[...] a child for 7[...]
When you[...] achieve, you'll[...] twisted doesn't [...]

Tyra Henry in hospital shortly before her death. The report of the inquiry into her death states that she "was at risk from the moment she was conceived"

Earlier reports failed

News of the World, February 12, 1984

WHAT A CRYING SHAME

NEWS of the WORLD
CAMPAIGN

GARY—Gashed by a thrown shoe

PETER—Burned by his father's cigarette

TRACY—Scorred by electric cooker rings

THE DUKE and his family: He spends long hours away, working for the NSPCC

TAKE a good look at these horrific pictures of savagely injured children.

They are part of a collection the Duke of Westminster always carries with him.

He doesn't enjoy showing them around but he wants everyone to see them — in the hope they will be shocked into helping him.

As chairman of the appeals committee of the National Society for the Prevention of Cruelty to Children, the Duke is out to raise £12 million by the end of the year.

Tests

"If we do...
NSPCC coule...
he says.

Duke battles to raise £12 million

How you can help

Tracy had been playing with...

But tests showed the cleaner was harmless.

Injuries to baby Ann appeared to have been caused by her buttocks being immersed in scalding liquid.

When she was treated for this, X-rays revealed she had fractures of both upper arms.

Neither the NSPCC nor the court could find out how Ann's... was caused.

● GARY'S father three... a shoe at him—and the picture shows what it did

expelling cruelty inflicted on other helpless youngsters.

So the parents had to hide the cigarette every time that child was burned. That's the sort of thing we're up against.

I never realised the size of the problem before I became involved. It is a very difficult message to get across.

Nobody likes to see pictures of abused children in the newspapers.

burns to the skin, a cigarette will go out.

By the permits had to prioritise be"

It's time editors and television producers brought this to the notice of the public. We can no longer skirt round the problem. People must face up to these pictures.

Since the Duke became chairman of the appeal...

we treat animals in comparison. Where do our priorities lie?

is about a 300-mile trip. But I love what I'm doing.

"My wife and I have talked about the time involved and she understands.

In fact she is going to help raise funds. So is everyone from schoolchildren to big business and showbusiness stars.

One school the Duke visited in Middlesbrough, Cleveland, raised £7,000 in five years.

The Duke said: "The problem is that the NSPCC is... must be frightened to...

very poor images of themselves and find it difficult to form relationships," says Barry Graham, 25, who runs a child care unit in Wiltshire.

"They see themselves as worthless in many ways."

Any parent who ends up hitting their child should seek immediate help.

"If you reach this point talk to neighbours, friend or anyone," says Mr Graham.

HERE are six ways in which you can give crucial support to the NSPCC's cause.

SEND, give or help raise badly-needed cash — and remember, top in every £1 the society receives comes from donations.

URGE your firm to support the Centenary Appeal, or set up a Centurion Club in your work to raise £100 by holding a sponsored event.

MONEY apart — if you suspect a child in your neighbourhood is being maltreated don't hesitate to call the NSPCC.

ENCOURAGE youngsters to join the society's Give an Hour for a Child scheme, aimed at increasing their awareness of the problem.

makes a covenant to pay a set amount every year.

Spok...

In popular accounts, child-battering was an extreme phenomenon, quite separate from the normal relations between parents and children. According to the *News of the World*, the solution for such inadequate families was not the intervention of interfering and muddle-headed professionals, but families – better families in every sense of the word. Only they could charm away the horrors in the form of charitable donations and by the power of their own contrasting image. A picture of one of the richest men in Britain, the Duke of Westminster, together with his own family group, was juxtaposed with pictures of children damaged by their parents. 'Duke battles to raise £12 million' read the caption.

By the mid 1980s, concern about child-battering had been replaced by a series of major scandals concerning the sexual abuse of children, usually within their families. The tabloids continued to assert their disbelief and seek out wrongly accused parents, but in a bizarre reversal, this most secret of topics reached the most public of media. Not only was sexual abuse explored in public-service programmes – like Thames Television's 'Help!' – and current affairs slots, but it appeared as peak-time entertainment viewing. Esther Rantzen's 'Childwatch', broadcast on BBC1 in October 1986: 'I was never frightened of walking home alone in the dark or of being raped or mugged. I knew what was waiting for me at home was infinitely worse than that', was the quotation from an anonymous child which introduced the programme in the *Radio Times*. The programme took the unprecedented step of speaking directly to children and advising

Too frightened to tell? Make that call! Sue Cook and Esther Rantzen launch ChildLine

them how to protect themselves. Under the slogan 'Speak to someone who cares', the picture in the *Radio Times* showed a little girl calling for help by public telephone – appealing both out of the family circle and beyond the bureaucratic network of social workers and faceless state agencies. The charismatic television star appeared to be providing an alternative to the welfare model. The programme launched ChildLine, a free and confidential telephone help line for children, whose logo is a smiling and unthreatening telephone. After its first year of operation, ChildLine estimated that 8,000 calls were made daily, of which about 800 got through.

In these new – yet old – and shocking narratives of violence and illicit sexuality, the question arose as to who was responsible for undermining that confident image so perfectly represented by the Duke of Westminster. In many feminist publications of the early 1980s the answer was, unequivocally, the Fathers. This was the term used by Elizabeth Ward, in her book *Father/Daughter Rape*, as the collective description for those men in positions of authority – fathers, stepfathers, uncles, babysitters – who have abused girl children. She argued that incest is not separable from other forms of child abuse. It is simply an extension of 'a socially sanctioned sexuality that is coercive and unequal, committed by males against those weaker females who are available to them'. For Florence Rush in *The Best Kept Secret*, 'the family itself is an instrument of sexual and other forms of child abuse. The protector and the rapist are the same person.' Mary McLeod and Esther Saraga argued that 'Sex abuse happens in normal families, not deficient ones.' Far from being its negation, the ever-present fantasy of incest is an extension of power maintained through sexuality. It welds the happy family together, while it throws a shadow across every claim to perfection. The picture of a family may be favourably juxtaposed with pictures of physically damaged children, but the possibility of incest forces us to reassess the composition of the group itself. This view poses problems for an imagery which seeks to find ways of representing a child in a secure setting beyond the family group. Childwatch's little girl with the telephone was one such attempt.

The popular press aimed to preserve the image of the united family. For the journalists, the interfering professionals were to blame. They invented abuse where there was none and maliciously removed children from their families. '"My nightmare" by Vanessa aged 8' ran the headline in the *Daily Mail*. 'They said, Daddy has done something to you. I kept telling them there was nothing wrong. I got so tired of them not believing me.' The campaigns were for 'parents' rights' and for children to be 'set free' and returned home so that the family image could be restored. But even when reunited, those families could be photographed only from behind, as a negative of the familiar group.

The only narrative of child sexual abuse which meshes easily with other interlinking narratives of child and family centres on the sexualised image of the young girl. It is a narrative of seduction. 'Perhaps I stared at my father in a provocative way.' The subheading in bold type rephrased the wry comment from the young girl interviewed in the *News of the World* magazine. In the text her words are: 'Perhaps I wriggled my nappy at him in a provocative way.' The rewriting makes the ludicrous irony sound suddenly possible. The image of the adolescent girl, degraded and made available by

THE STAR

GOING HOME

RITAIN'S LIVELIEST DAILY   WEDNESDAY, JULY 1, 1987   **20p** (21p CIs)

ND IN HAND: Two little children walk away with their mum and dad last night after a judge in the Cleveland child sex abuse case ordered their release. For this
ily the ordeal was over . . . for now. But for other parents the nightmare goes on. Their youngsters must stay in care. **JOY AND DESPAIR: Pages 2 and 3.**

premature sexual experience, is the only image to accompany features on child abuse in which the young person is regularly shown, looking directly at the viewer. Aware of her sexuality, she can be accused of provoking assault. Faced with this pressure from the image, the first incest survivors to speak out could hardly trust themselves. 'No one knows the inner torment I feel. I'm racked with guilt in case I provoked it. I'm a freak!' wrote 'Liz' in the *Leveller* magazine.

The image of the girl child alone remains the most striking of contrasts with the image of the happy family group, for she signals that the innocence of childhood is always deceptive. She holds immeasurable dangers for adult men. Her seductiveness may provoke them into betraying their dignity, and what is more, she knows their terrible secret. After all, Freud's first moves towards developing his theory of the Oedipus complex came when, in the mid 1890s, he decided that his women patients' memories of paternal abuse in their infancy were based on a universal fantasy. His intuitions were confirmed, he wrote, when he recognised his *own* ambivalent feelings towards his daughter. In the theory, the incestuous desires of the father were superseded by the Oedipal longings of the son. Either way, the position of the man at the apex of the family group is

A bright girl of 18, Jackie has thick dark hair and a smattering of freckles. She loves listening to her rock music, putting on outrageous clothes and trying out all the latest make-up colours. She is just like any other happy, normal teenager. Or would be, if it wasn't for one fact. A few months ago, Jackie sent her father to prison where he is now serving five years for incest.

Jackie looks quite relaxed—but she has tried to kill herself several times. Now the only way she can hold herself together emotionally, and look towards a more cheerful and normal future, is by trying to "blot out" most of her childhood, with the help of two years' psychiatric therapy. It's her only path to happiness and peace of mind—her only hope.

What sort of father could do such a thing to his own daughter? That's the question Jackie's tragic story makes us all ask. Until recently, the very word incest was taboo in our society. But today the shocking truth is that it is being uncovered more and more frequently, in all walks of life. And teachers, social workers and other adults in charge of children are wising up on the signs to look out for—the strange aches and pains, the bed-wetting, sudden retreat into a fantasy world and obvious distress—that could mean a child is being sexually molested at home.

Surveys have shown that behind those outwardly respectable front doors, one in 10 British homes now shelters a sex offender and at least one child victim, along with untold mental and physical anguish.

The law defines incest as sexual

"At three years old, you don't know what's wrong – perhaps I stared at my father in a provocative way"

intercourse between any people who are so closely related that they would not legally be allowed to marry. Other organisations define it more widely as "any sexual contact between a child and an adult in a position of trust". Most frequently, it is father-daughter incest cases that come before the courts or to the attention of social workers and the medical profession, but there is increasing evidence that

INCEST

A tragedy of innocent lives scarred and childhoods lost forever – incest is the taboo subject no one likes to talk about. But in one out of every 10 British homes it is happening today. Report by Ellen Petrie

"I hate my dad for what he did to me"

always under threat. He is exposed as capable of provoking total disruption at just that point where he claims to be the upholder of rationality and order.

The ongoing debates around child abuse have raised the issue of childhood sexuality, only to declare it an impossible topic. A climate has been created where the exploration of children's sexuality – or even sensuality – seems possible only under conditions of exploitation, or else is deemed unspeakable. But the imagery of childhood is never without its ambiguities. The danger to children is balanced by an all-pervasive sense of a danger from them. Children, in all their enforced irrationality, pose a threat to adults, both in their own tendency to violence and lack of control and in their ability to provoke adults to violence and loss of control. In popular narratives, the newspaper accounts of young boys who rejoice in cruelty are only a few steps away from the threatening young tyrants of the consumer advertisements. In the advertisements children's demands may test their parents' patience, but things are never allowed to go too far. The child may never disrupt the stable, consuming family. Instead they can be seen teasing their parents, developing strategies to exploit their imposed dependence, using their knowledge to display a lack of knowledge, and recognising their hold over adults. Their refusal to conform and their ability to drive adults crazy are compounded by their knowing provocativeness. In their pioneering work on child abuse, Henry and Ruth Kempe point out that some abused children may become 'demon children': negative, aggressive, hyperactive. It is difficult to get away from a feeling that this potential of childhood should be kept down at any cost. A fear of the unmanageable child merges into a fear of the diabolical child, with power to overturn the order of social life. This image can be fully expressed only in fictional characters – in films like *The Exorcist; Damien: The Omen; Carrie* – where children exercise demonic and destructive powers. Adult love of children is accompanied by adult hatred of children and adult fear of children's hatred.

The image of violent children is complementary to that of children who have been violently treated. Violence against children is a secret, spoken of with difficulty, yet it remains the ultimate threat, built into the structuring of difference between adult and child. Images of violence are necessary to express the fear we feel; actual violence is the cost of an order based on domination and exclusion. The unstable state of childhood in itself provokes the fear which is so visible in the imagery – fear of the incomprehensibility and uncontrollability of real children and fear of the unconquered child within our adult selves. Forms of control which seem necessary to subjugate a dangerous irruption of childhood in effect suppress and humiliate actual children.

Conclusion
Escape from childhood

Pictures of children are made in a world which sees childhood as a precious quality which may be stolen or wantonly rejected. Since children are open to exploitation, some argue that their childishness must be protected above all other considerations. Yet the bitter experience of being a child is a continuous struggle to escape from childhood, to leave behind precisely those qualities of simplicity, ignorance and innocence that are so highly valued.

Like everyone else, children live in a world of meanings. They, too, respond to the imagery that surrounds us all, making use of it to define themselves and their experiences. Yet of all social groups, children are the least able to explore their view of themselves in the public domain. To be a child is not to inhabit the mythical dreamland of the imagery but to be a thinking, acting individual, with the ability to make sense of the material to hand. Living through childhood means coping with continuous change. The child's own body undergoes rapid transformations, and social definitions change with it. Adult expectations of a growing child's behaviour, appearance and demeanour are constantly readjusted, but adult consciousness seems unwilling to embrace such instability. Instead of drawing on this rich resource, the imagery seeks to impose its own nervous limits.

If children had greater access to a public voice, if they were able to contribute to the social meanings with which we make sense of our world, the result would not be a more 'childish' set of images. Rather, we would be forced to readjust our concept of childhood, and our notion of what it means to be an adult would necessarily become more flexible. Children should, perhaps, be heard as much as they are seen. We could then expect an even richer pleasure from the image.

THE CONVENTION ON THE RIGHTS OF THE CHILD

gives legal force to the human rights of every child, regardless of race, colour, sex, disability, national, ethnic or social background, or economic circumstance.

Children's rights can be grouped in four essential categories:

SURVIVAL
Every child has a right to nourishing food, clean water and effective health care.

DEVELOPMENT
Every child has a right to develop to his or her full potential, loved, cared for, and afforded every opportunity to learn and to play.

PROTECTION
Every child has a right to protection from war and from any form of violence, from mental, physical and sexual abuse, from exploitative work and abandonment.

PARTICIPATION
Every child has a right to a name and nationality, a right to have his or her opinions taken into account, and a right to participate, more fully with increasing maturity, in all the activities of society.

UNICEF *The State of the World's Children*

every picture tells a story

The Gu
all form
commu
aim to
repres
Save th
interna
externa
include

● adv
televisi
newsp
magaz
and dir

● pub
press r
statem
publica
educat
display
public
talks, s
fundra
promot
partner
reports
and vid

Everyo
promot
Childre
the Gui
volunte
membe
partner

175

References

Introduction

Page 9

Walter Benjamin, 'The Work of Art in the Age of Mechanical Reproduction', in *Illuminations*, Fontana, 1973, p. 224 (written in 1936).

Page 14

Mary Whitehouse, 'Today's children *are* deprived – of their childhood!', *Daily Express*.

Page 16

Bernard Fearnley, *Child Photography*, 1972, p. 87.

Page 18

Roland Barthes, 'Rhetoric of the Image', in *Image, Music, Text*, Fontana, 1977, p. 34 (first published 1964).

Page 19

Paul Goodman, *Growing up Absurd*, Sphere, 1970 (first published 1956 in USA).

Page 20

Judith Ennew, *The Sexual Exploitation of Children*, Polity Press, 1986.

1 There's no such thing as a baby . . .

Page 22

D.W. Winnicott, *The Child, The Family and The Outside World*, Pelican, 1964, p. 88.

Page 24

Val Williams, *Women Photographers*, Virago, 1986, p. 141 discusses Grace Robertson's childbirth pictures.

Page 27

Frédérick Leboyer, *Birth Without Violence*, Fontana, 1977.

Page 29

British Medical Association, *You and Your Baby*, 1981, p. 5.

Page 30

Marina Warner, *Alone of All Her Sex*, Picador, 1985, p. 183.

Page 31

Dr Shelagh Tyrrell, *You and Your Baby*, BMA, 1976.
Sheila Kitzinger, 'The Psychology of Breastfeeding', in *Breastfeeding: A Challenge for Midwives*, Melbourne, International Council of Midwives, 1984.

Page 32

Cow and Gate advertisement by Abbott Mead, *Campaign*, 19 May 1989.
Dinah Hall, 'When milking profits breast isn't best', *The Sunday Correspondent*, 26 November 1989.

Page 33

Edward Vale, *Daily Mirror*, 5 August 1982.
The Baby Book, Charing Cross Hospital Obstetrics Department, 1980.

Page 34

Benjamin Spock, *Baby and Childcare*, first published in USA 1944.
Martin Richards interviewed by Christina Hardyment, 'And were you breast-fed yourself, Dr Jolly?', *Observer*, 14 April 1985.

Page 35

Penelope Leach, *Baby and Child*, Penguin, 1979, p. 16.

Page 36

Tony Osman, 'Survival of the cutest', *Sunday Times*, 21 August 1977.

Page 38

'Image of Love', *Mother*, July 1978, discusses photographs of babies in intensive care.
Gail Kemp, 'Shock tactics that produce great ads', *Campaign*, 25 March 1988.
Kevin Pilley, 'Ad world gives birth to baby power', *Campaign*, 6 January 1990.
Truby King was quoted by Sheila Kitzinger, *Independent Magazine*, 5 May 1990.

Page 40

Time-Life, *Photographing Children*, 1973, pp. 92–3.
John Hegarty was quoted by Sarah Mower, 'Macho man gives way to caring father', *Independent*, 6 November 1989.

2 Superbrats in the charmed circle of home

Page 53

Annalena McAfee, 'The brat race', *Evening Standard*, 1 August 1988.

Page 55

Royal Society for the Prevention of Accidents was quoted by Bryony Coleman and Jenny Cowley, 'What is your little treasure worth?', *Mail on Sunday*, 3 December 1989.

Page 57

Martin Wroe, 'Hello! Here's a nice little earner', *Independent*, 10 July 1991.

Page 58

Lesley Garner and Ivor Davis, 'The proxy fathers: sowing the seeds of despair?', *Sunday Times Magazine*.

3 Ignorant pupils and harmonious nature

Page 60

C.B. Cox and A.E. Dyson (eds), *Fight for Education: a Black Paper*, Critical Quarterly Society, 1968.

Page 61

Central Office of Information, *Education Reform in Britain*, 1989, speaks of the needs of an 'advanced technological country' in its introduction to the 1988 Education Reform Act.
Richard Johnson *et al.*, *Unpopular Education*, Hutchinson, 1982, p. 26.

Page 64

Michel Foucault, *Discipline and Punish*, Allen Lane, 1977, p. 143.

Page 67

J. M. Bynner, quoted in *Unpopular Education*, p. 35.
The Plowden Committee, *Children and their Primary Schools*, HMSO, 1966, para 523.

Page 69

Maria Montessori, *The Secret of Childhood*, Longman, 1936, p. 189.

Page 70

Joanna Patyna, 'What are they learning now?', *Evening News*, 9 May 1978.

Page 78

'Please sir, don't be trendy', *Daily Mirror*, 26 April 1976.
'Ivory classrooms', *Sun*, 29 July 1975.

Page 80

Colin McCabe, *Independent* 9, December 1990, wrote of the changes in the aspiration to an egalitarian education.

4 The fantasy of liberation and the demand for rights

Page 82

Marie-José Lérés-Richer, 'The Child at Play', *Forum*, Council of Europe, February 1979.
Time-Life, *Photographing Children*, Time-Life International, 1971, p. 138.
Leila Berg, *Look at Kids*, Penguin, 1972.

Page 85

Eglantyne Jebb, quoted by Yvonne Roberts in 'The Rights of the Child', *Observer*, 30 September 1990.

Page 86

Leila Berg, *Kids*, no. 1., 1972.
Everett Reimer, *School is Dead*, Penguin, 1971.
John Holt, *Escape from Childhood*, Penguin, 1975.
A.S. Neill, *That Dreadful School*, Jenkins, 1937.
Ivan Illich, *Deschooling Society*, Calder & Boyars, 1971.
Paulo Freire, *The Pedagogy of the Oppressed*, Penguin, 1972.

Page 87

Dave Freeman wrote about the dilemmas of being a teacher in *Rank and File*, no. 23,
Winter 1972.

Page 92

Paul Adams, 'The Infant, The Family and Society', in Paul Adams *et al.*, *Children's
Rights*, Elek, 1971.

Page 93

Adams, in *Children's Rights*, p. 79.
Keith Paton, *Kids*, no. 1, 1972.

Page 95

Colin Ward, *The Child and the City*, Architectural Press, 1977.

Page 96

Robert Franklin, *The Rights of Children*, Blackwell, 1986.

Page 98

UNICEF, *The Girl Child: An Investment in the Future*, revised edition, 1991.

5 No future: The impossibility of youth

Page 100

John Downing and Tom Smith, 'Day trip to terror', *Daily Express*, 8 April 1980.
Mark Abrams, *The Teenage Consumer*, London Press Exchange, 1959.
Rufus Olins, 'Enter the superbrats, children of the 90s', *Observer*, 7 October 1990,
discusses the report *Spoilt Brats*.

Page 101

India Knight, 'The teenage rebel is dead', *Campaign*, 13 May 1988.

Page 102

Marje Proops, 'The savage generation', *Daily Mirror*, 19 September 1977.

Page 104

Police officer quoted in 'Day trip to terror'.

Page 105

'Bloody kids', *Daily Mirror*, 25 April 1983.

Page 106

Roland Barthes, *The Pleasure of the Text*, Jonathan Cape, 1976, pp. 3–4.

Page 107

Dick Hebdige, *Hiding in the Light*, Routledge, 1988.
T.R. Fyvel, *The Insecure Offenders*, Pelican, 1963, p. 36.

Page 108

Daily Star, 26 May 1980.
Ian Jack, *Sunday Times Magazine*, November 1981.

Page 109

'Despair', *The Face*, no. 65, September 1985, p. 73.

Page 110

Sid Vicious interviews: *Daily Mirror*, 11 June 1977 and 19 December 1977.

Page 111

Charlie: *Daily Mirror*, 8 April 1980.
'The junk generation', *Daily Mirror*, 4 December 1985.

Page 113

'What's the matter with kids today?' *Daily Mirror*, 31 July 1978, was a sympathetic view of unemployed youth.

Page 114

News of the World, 21 November 1982.
'Just William', *Daily Mail*, 13 October 1977.

Page 117

'Aggro Britain', *Sun*, 26 August 1980.
Sunday Mirror, 12 July 1981.

Page 118

'Arrogant hooligans' described the student demonstration at Essex University: *Evening Standard*, 8 April 1974.
'Stunted demons' described street riots in Liverpool 8: Brian James, *Daily Mail*, 8 July 1981.
'St Paul's: revolt of the lost tribe', *Observer*, 6 April 1980.
'Not England': *Daily Express*, 7 October 1985.
Jean Richie, *Sun*, 11 November 1980.

Page 120

'The shape of things to come', *Daily Mirror*, 13 April 1981.
Jeff Edwards, 'If you know 'em, Shop 'Em', *The People*, 13 May 1990.

Page 121

'Rough justice', *Daily Mail*, 13 August 1976.

6 Sex and sexuality

Page 122

Stephen Heath, *The Sexual Fix*, Macmillan, 1982, p. 141.
Sara Stein, *Boys and Girls*, Chatto & Windus, 1984.

Page 123

Karen Farrington, 'Would you buy your son a doll?', *Woman*, 20 December 1988.

Page 126

Erving Goffman, *Gender Advertisements*, Macmillan, 1979.

Page 127

Heath, *The Sexual Fix*, p. 139.

Page 129

Luce Irigaray, quoted by Toril Moi in *Sexual/Textual Politics*, Methuen, 1985, pp. 139–40.

Page 130

Toy retailer Gerry Masters was quoted by Karen Farrington in 'Would you buy your son a doll?'.

Page 134

Shan Lancaster, 'Sam, 16, quits A-levels of Ooh-levels!', *Sun*, 22 February 1983. Goffman, *Gender Advertisements*.

Page 138

On Brooke Shields: *Sun*, 3 June 1985.
On Jodie Foster: Brian Wesley, 'Sweet sixteen', *Daily Star*, 16 February 1979.
Victor Davis, 'The O-level cover girls', *Mail on Sunday*, 30 August 1987.
On Milla Jovovich: Glenn O'Brien, 'Milla Dollar Baby', *Sunday Times Magazine*, 1988.
Barbara Jones, *Mail on Sunday*, 24 August 1987.

Page 140

Gail Kemp, 'Shock tactics that produce great ads', *Campaign*, 25 March 1988.

Page 141

Fifteen-year-old model, quoted by Victor Davis in 'The O-level cover girls'.
Geraldine Bedell, 'This girl is for sale . . .', *Independent on Sunday*, 22 July 1990.

Page 144

Corinna Honan, 'The Dilemma of Schoolgirl Mothers', *Woman*, 1980.

Page 145

'Making love in the corridors', *Daily Express*, February 1980.

Page 146

Florence Rush, *The Best Kept Secret*, Prentice Hall, New Jersey, 1980.

7 Crybabies and damaged children

Page 151

Paul Harrison and Robin Palmer, *News Out of Africa*, Hilary Shipman, 1986, p. 97.

Page 153

'Moved to give', *Guardian*, 17 August 1982.

Page 155

Teresa Hayter, 'Aid: The West's False Handout', *New Socialist* 24, February 1985.
Within Human Reach, UNICEF, 1985.

Page 156

Ogilvy and Mather, quoted in the *Guardian*.
J. Walter Thompson in *'Open Space'*, BBC 1 June 1991.

Page 157

Richard Dowden, 'Dying by Darwinian logic', *Independent*, 17 July 1991.

Page 158

'Mirror to the rescue', *Daily Mirror*, 27 October 1984.
'Face of hope', *Daily Mail*, 13 May 1991.

Page 161

UN estimates of children bearing arms quoted by Alessandra Stanley, 'Child Warriors', *Time International*, 18 June 1990.
For an account of sex tourism, see Judith Ennew, *The Sexual Exploitation of Children*, Polity, 1986, p. 97.

Page 162

'Socially acceptable': *Guardian*, 3 April 1991.
Zoe Heller, *Independent on Sunday*, 5 May 1991.
Alice Miller, *Thou Shalt Not Be Aware*, Pluto, 1985, p. 192.

Page 164

Anthea Gerrie, 'Should it be illegal to smack your own child?', *Daily Mail*, 20 April 1989.

Page 165

Beatrice and Ronald Gross (eds), *The Children's Rights Movement*, Doubleday Anchor, New York, 1977.
Lloyd de Mause, *The History of Childhood*, Souvenir, 1976.
Miller, *Thou Shalt Not Be Aware*.

Page 166

D. Bakan, *The Slaughter of the Innocents*, Jossey-Bass, San Francisco, 1971.

Page 167

Home Office Chief Medical Officer quoted in Selwyn M. Smith, *The Battered Child Syndrome*, Butterworth, 1975.

Page 170

Elizabeth Ward, *Father/Daughter Rape*, Women's Press, 1984.
Florence Rush, *The Best Kept Secret*, Prentice Hall, New Jersey, 1980.
Mary McLeod and Esther Saraga, 'Abuse of Trust', *Marxism Today*, August 1987.
Roger Scott, '"My nightmare" by Vanessa aged 8', *Daily Mail*, 23 June 1988.

Page 172

Ellen Petrie, 'Incest', *News of the World Magazine*.
Liz, 'Too afraid to speak', *Leveller*, no. 78, 2–15 April, 1982.
Sigmund Freud, discussed by Florence Rush in 'The Great Freudian Cover Up,' *Touble and Strife* 4, Winter 1984.

Page 173

Henry and Ruth Kempe, *Child Abuse*, Fontana, 1978, p. 50.

Illustration Credits

Every effort has been made to trace copyright holders in all copyright material in this book. The author regrets any errors or omissions that may inadvertantly remain.

Page 13
Woman's Own, 28 May 1988. Photograph: Sandra Lousado/Susan Griggs Agency.

Page 15
Advertisements for: Heinz Sandwich Spread, late 1970s,
Franklin Mint Ltd., late 1980s Painting: Margaret Keane.

Page 17
Cover of *Amateur Photographer*, 14 September 1977.
Reply-paid envelope for film developing service.
Advertisements for: Halina Cameras, early 1980s.
Kodak Pocket A1 Camera, late 1970s.
Ron Oliver, child photographer, 1988.

Page 20
Daily Mirror, 19 September 1972. Photograph: Charles Ley.

Page 23
Advertisement for Children's World Superstore, 1990s.

Page 24/5
Photo sequence from *Parents*, April 1976.

Page 26
Photograph from Frédérick Leboyer, *Birth Without Violence*, Fontana, 1977, I.M.S. Stockholm.
Cover of Adam Suddaby's *The Nuclear War Game*, Longman, 1983.

Page 28
Covers of: *Woman*, 4 February 1984.
Mother and Baby, February 1992.
Tatler, September 1990.
Advertisement for Murphy Radios, late 1970s.

Page 29
Health Education Council leaflet, mid 1970s.
Mothercare Catalogue, 1989.
Logo of the National Childbirth Trust.

Page 30
Christmas cards, current from the 1970s to the 1990s.

Page 32
Advertisements for: Cow and Gate Baby Food, Abbott Mead, 1983.
Cannon Babysafe products, early 1980s.

Page 33
'Congratulations' card: Freedom Greetings, US, 1980s.
Leaflet for Cow and Gate, late 1980s.

Page 34/5
Drawings from *Now you're a family*, Health Education Council, 1979.

Page 36
From 'Survival of the cutest', *Sunday Times*, 21 August 1977. Drawings: Sally Launder
© Times Newspapers Limited, 1977.

Page 37
Congratulations Card: Royale Publications, 1970s Designer: Glükli.
Advertisement for Milk Marketing Board, early 1980s.
Leaflet for Maws Ltd., 1980s.
Cover of *Baby Magazine*, late Spring 1991. Photograph: Lesley Howling. Model:
Theodora Kingston. Clothes: Next Directory.
Package for Cow and Gate Babymilk Plus, late 1970s.

Page 39
Advertisements for: Johnson and Johnson nappy liners, 1980.
Asilone Pharmaceuticals, late 1970s.
Molivate, Glaxo, late 1970s.

Page 41
Advertisements for: Halifax Building Society, late 1970s.
Mercantile Credit, 1988.
The Times, Saturday Review, 1990.

Page 42
Advertisement for Haliborange, 1991.

Page 43
Today, 25 August 1990.

Page 45
Leaflet for DHSS: Family Income Supplement, November 1977.
Annual Report: Nationwide Building Society, 1980.
Advertisement for Creative Knitters Club, late 1970s.
Mail on Sunday: You magazine offer, 1991.

Page 48
News of the World, 8 January 1978.
Daily Mirror, 14 September 1989.

Page 49
Advertisement for De Beers diamonds, early 1970s.
Leaflet for Midland Bank Access Card and Accident and Disability Protection, 1980.

Page 50
Leaflet for DHSS: Family Income Supplement, November 1978.
Leaflet for Barclays Insurance Services, mid 1970s.

Page 51
Advertisement for Pakistan International Airways, early 1980s.
Catalogue for Green Shield Stamps, early 1970s.

Page 53
Catalogue for Mothercare, 1989.

Page 54
Advertisement for Levis Youth Wear, late 1970s.

Page 55
Advertisement for Woolworths 'Streets Ahead' children's clothing, 1988.

Page 56
Advertisement for Cadbury's Dairy Milk chocolate, late 1970s.

Page 57
Postcard of the Royal Family, mid 1980s. Colorama Ltd. Photograph: Tim Graham.

Page 58
Observer 10 February 1991. Photograph: Christopher Moore.
Cover of *Lifestyle*, Winter 1990.

Page 59
Advertisement for Volvo 440 Turbo, early 1990s.

Page 61
Parents, 1975. Photograph: Graham Henderson.
Cover of *Mother*, September 1983. Photograph: Jeany.

Page 65
Photographs from: *Guardian*, August 1983.
                  South London Press, 24 November 1987.
                  Guardian, 9 February 1988, Ed Sirrs.
                  Guardian, 3 May 1988, Azadour Gazelian.
                  Guardian, 25 January 1991, Don McPhee.

Page 66
Leaflet for 345 Nursery Course, early 1980s.

Page 68
Page from *ILEA Contact*, Issue 21, 1974.

Page 71
Kentish Times: 6 October 1983, Photographs: Ken Watt.
                  10 October 1983, Photographs: Don Reed.

Page 72
Catalogue for Open University audio tapes, 1976.
Advertisement for BASF, 1974.
National Union of Teachers, *Secondary Education*, November 1977.
Department of Education and Science, *National Curriculum Guide*, 1990.

Page 73
Advertisement for Trent Plan, early 1970s.
Package for Kelloggs Sultana Bran, mid 1980s.
Booklet for National Extension College Teaching Course, 1972.

Page 74
Observer, 22 February 1981.

Page 77
Advertisements for: Peter Lord shoes, 1980.
Woolworths school clothes, 1986.
Abbey Life insurance, 1980.

Page 79
Advertisement for *Teaching as a Career Information Pack*, 1991.

Page 80
Daily Mirror, 22 May 1972.
Daily Mirror, 28 February 1990.

Page 83
Cover of *Forum*, Council of Europe, February 1971.
Leaflet on *Children's Rights*, 1991. Photograph: Prodeepta Das.
'Guide to the Children Act', *Community Care*, April, 1990. Photograph: John Birdsall.

Page 84
Cover of *Peace News*, 30 May 1975.

Page 87
Cover of *Libertarian Teacher*, No. 7, July 1971.

Page 89
Cover of *Libertarian Education*, No. 11, April 1973.
Timetable from *Y-Front*, No. 3, 1972.
Caged heads from *Radical Education*, No. 2, Winter 1974/5.

Page 90/91
Y-Front, No. 3, 1972.

Page 92
Covers of: *Children's Rights*, No. 1, 1972. Design: Pearce Marchbank.
Martin Hoyles (ed), *Changing Childhood*, Writers and Readers, 1979. Design:
Bolivar.

Page 93
Cover of *Undercurrents*, 36 October/November 1979.

Page 94
from *Children's Rights*, No. 3, 1973.

Page 95
Guardian, 9 July 1986.

Page 97
NSPCC, 1989.

Page 98/99
UNICEF–UK, 1991. Design: Bob Pascall.

Page 101
Daily Express 8 April 1980. Photographs: John Downing.

Page 102
Daily Mirror, 19 September 1977.

Page 103
News of the World, 21 November 1982.

Page 105
Daily Mirror, 25 April 1983.

Page 106
Daily Star, 29 May 1980. Photograph: Simon Pythian.

Page 108
Covers of: *No. 1*, 7 September 1985.
            Just 17, 11 September 1985.

Page 109
Covers of:*Etcetera*, 13 September 1985.
i-D, December/January 1986.

Page 110
Daily Mirror, 3 February 1979.

Page 111
Daily Mirror, 4 December 1985.

Page 112
Advertisement for Manpower Services Commission, Youth Opportunities
Programme, 1978.

Page 113
Daily Express, 20 April 1989. Photographs: John Downing.

Page 115
Hammersmith Chronicle, 1 July 1977. Photograph: Kemp.
Daily Mail, 13 October 1977.

Page 116
Observer, 24 January 1982. Photograph: Derek Millward.
Observer Magazine, 24 February 1985. Photograph: Mike Abrahams.

Page 117
Daily Mail, 8 July 1981. Photograph: Barry Farrell.

Page 119
Daily Mirror, 13 April 1981.
Sunday Mirror, 1 April 1990. Photographs: Les Wilson, John Shenton, Samantha
Pearce, Dale Cherry, Graham Sutch and Paul Webb.

Page 120
Evening News, 17 May 1972.
Daily Mirror, 3 March 1981. Photograph: Alisdair Macdonald.

Page 121
The Sun, 11 July 1981.
Observer, 21 October 1990. Photograph: Daniel White.

Page 123
'Congratulations' cards: Sharpes Classics, 1980s.

Page 124
Observer Magazine 5 November 1978. Illustration: Dick Bruna © Copyright Mercis bv 1978.

Page 126
Two advertisements for Heinz Beans, late 1970s.

Page 127
Two advertisements for Playskool toys, late 1980s.

Page 128
Two advertisements for Nesquik milk-shake mix, mid 1980s.
Woman, 25 October 1988. Photograph: Paul Dunn.

Page 129
Leaflet for Cheese Bureau, mid 1970s.
Advertisement for Electricity Council, mid 1970s.

Page 130
Fashion spread in *Observer Magazine*, 23 October 1977. Photographs: Christina Peters.

Page 131
Advertisement for K shoes, mid 1980s.

Page 132
Illustration from Ladybird Books, 1970s.
Birthday card, 1980s.

Page 133
Advertisement for Life Offices Association, late 1960s.
Guardian, 1979.
Sunday Mirror, 5 May 1991.

Page 134
Daily Mirror, 22 February 1983. Photographs: John Paul and David White.

Page 135
Advertisement for Clarks shoes, late 1970s.

Page 136
Advertisements for: *Elle*, May 1985.
                   Marks and Spencer, 1988.
Fashion spread from *Observer Magazine*, 1978. Photographs: James Wedge.

Page 137
Knitting patterns from: *Family Circle*, April 1988 and May 1988.
                        Woman's Own, May 1988.
Advertisement for Cussons Imperial Leather deodorant, 1988.

Page 139
Advertisement for Graff jewellery, late 1980s.

Page 140
Advertisement for Cow and Gate Baby Foods, Abbott Mead Vickers/SMS, 1988.

Page 142
Guardian, 15 June 1978.

Page 143
Advertisement for Rufus Murray Mail Order Clothing, 1979.

Page 144
Sun, 26 September 1979.

Page 145
Sun, 25 April 1991. Photograph: Roger Crump, Clothes: Youngs Pronuptia.
Today, 23 February 1987. Photograph: Mike Lawn.

Page 146
Birthday card: Angel Cards, 1980s.
Christmas card: 1980s.
Catalogue for Early Learning, Spring/Summer 1980.

Page 147
Advertisement for Kids Klobber clothing at Asda Superstores, 1985.

Page 149
Advertisements for: Christian Aid, early 1980s.
                    Action Aid, early 1990s.
                    Action in Distress, late 1970s.
Guardian, 18 December 1982.

Page 151
Guardian, 27 November 1981.
Sunday Correspondent, 29 January 1990. Photograph: Stuart Nicol.

Page 152
Daily Star, 8 May 1991.

Page 153
Advertisement for Save the Children, early 1980s.

Page 154
Cover of *New Internationalist*, January 1987.
Pamphlet for War on Want, 1979.
Advertisement for War on Want, 1987.

Page 156
Save the Children, *Focus on Images*, 1991.

Page 157
Advertisement for Action Aid, 1981.
Cover of *Sunday Express Magazine*, 19 May 1991.

Page 158
Daily Mail, 13 May 1991. Photograph: Freddy Rikken.

Page 159
Daily Mirror, 11 July 1977.

Page 160
Sunday Mirror, 1 June 1986.
Cover of Morris Fraser's *Children in Conflict*, Penguin, 1973. Photograph: Clive Limpkin.
Guardian, 29 April 1988. Photograph: Caroline Penn.

Page 161
Independent on Sunday, 5 May 1991. Photograph: Ben Gibson/Impact Photos.

Page 163
Daily Mirror, 19 September 1972.

Page 165
Daily Mirror, 16 June 1977.
Advertisements for: NSPCC, 1979.
National Children's Homes, 1989.

Page 167
Advertisement for NSPCC, 1984.
Guardian, 19 December 1987.

Page 168
News of the World, 12 February 1984.

Page 169
Advertisement for *Childwatch* BBC1 30 October 1986. Photograph: Judy Goodhill.
Logo for Childline, launched 1986.

Page 171
Star, 1 July 1987.

Page 172
News of the World Magazine, early 80s. Photograph: Conrad Hafenrichter.

Page 175
UNICEF. UK, 1991.
Save the Children, *Focus on Images*, 1991.

Also of interest

FAMILY SNAPS: The Meanings of Domestic Photography

Edited by Jo Spence and Patricia Holland

Memories are made of this – the family album, the most personal and popular of photographic collections. Parents posed for a formal portrait, children lined up on the beach: snapshots and professional portraits adhere to the accepted rules, and yet they hold secret meanings shared only by an intimate circle. To the outsider, the album may be a social document; to those pictured on its pages, the images may reverberate with complex memories and emotions.

In this illuminating and original collection of writings and photographs, as well as photographic essays, twenty-five contributors – among them Wendy Ewald, Stuart Hall, Annette Kuhn, Jeremy Seabrook, Adeola Solanke, Jo Spence, Simon Watney and Val Williams – look at the many and shifting meanings of domestic photography. Among their concerns are the transformation of the family album into narratives of community, religion, ethnicity and nation; the consequence of a changing technology on changing images; questions of identity; and phototherapy as a way of exploring the self. This is a fascinating reading of images, between the lines and against the grain.